# Moving the Church in 7 STEPs

# Moving the Church in 7 STEPs

*(Strategic, Targeted, Evangelistic Plans)*

### David B. Newell

Copyright © 2017 – David B. Newell

All rights reserved. No part of this book may be used or reproduced in any manner, stored in a retrieval system, or transmitted in any form or by any means—electronic, mechanical, photocopy, recording, scanning or any other—except in the case of brief quotations in printed reviews, without the prior written permission from the author. Scripture quotations are taken from THE HOLY BIBLE, NEW INTERNATIONAL VERSION®, NIV® Copyright © 1973, 1978, 1984, 2011 by Biblica, Inc.™ Used by permission. All rights reserved worldwide. Emphasis within Scripture is the author's own.

Scotland Media Group
3583 Scotland Road, Building 70
Scotland PA 17254

Book ISBN: 978-1-941746-36-3
eBook ISBN: 978-1-941746-37-0

For Worldwide Distribution
Printed in the United States

1 2 3 4 5 6 7 / 21 20 19 18 17

# Dedication

This book is dedicated to all the saints, past and present, who have felt the call of God on their lives, and dared to step into the arena to make a difference in the lives of others by introducing them to Jesus Christ. To all of those who entered the arena to fight the good fight, to name the name of Christ and suffer persecution, hardship, poverty, brokenness and despair, all so others could be counted among the followers of Christ, I salute you.

# Contents

| | |
|---|---:|
| Introduction It Is Time | ix |
| 1 Strategic, Targeted, Evangelistic Plans | 1 |
| 2 Societal and Cultural Battlefields | 19 |
| 3 Step by Step | 37 |
| 4 Step One: Strategic Foundation | 55 |
| 5 Step Two: Targeted Audience | 111 |
| 6 Step Three: Evangelistic Strategies | 121 |
| 7 Step Four: Planned Strategies | 131 |
| 8 Step Five: Teamwork | 137 |
| 9 Step Six: Executing Effective Tactics | 143 |
| 10 Step Seven: Review and Improve | 147 |
| Conclusion | 151 |
| Appendix A About Catalytic Leadership Academy | 155 |
| Appendix B Scripture Passages Cited | 159 |
| Endnotes | 161 |
| Bibliography | 169 |
| About the Author | 175 |

# Introduction

# It Is Time

It is time for the Church, believers as a whole worldwide, to engage and lead the dialogue on every topic confronting culture. There are always those who try to shout the Church down, and in the recent past, we accommodated them. Those days are over.

Not every exchange is going to be a picture of healthy debate, because many people do not want that. While reason is important, Scripture has already spoken, and it is supreme and the ultimate source against which all else is measured. History is full of personalities who have done their best to undermine the authority of Scripture as the legitimate foundation upon which good society is built. But for we Christians, Scripture is the final authority.

Scripture is the divine special revelation and the means by which God has communicated His desires for His children. The Church must never allow those not in the Church to define the narrative of what is or is not proper engagement for the Church. Even some within the Church think the world is cookies and rainbows. That level of naïveté is astounding. So too is the behavior of some within the Church to embrace the values of current cultural winds over and above the teachings of Scripture.

Foundational to this book's premise, is the commitment to the inspiration, infallible, authority of the Bible as the Word of God.

We are in a spiritual battle that manifests first in that realm, and if the saints are not sufficiently engaged at that level, the battle spills over and manifests elsewhere. There is good and there is evil. We have *the* message for humanity. It is our call to bring it. There will be those who hate us for it, but that goes with the territory.

Time to suit up, put on the armor, and be ready for battle at every level and in every domain.

This book is both a commentary and a guide. The central point is to determine the processes by which the Church, and specifically a single congregation of believers, might move forward without fear, and with great courage and boldness toward greater effectiveness. It assumes that a complete organizational assessment and strategic plan has been developed, and the Seven Steps function as a subset to that plan.

## Evangelism

The field of evangelism, in particular, is the logical place to begin our journey to bring about Kingdom impact. It represents the direction Christ gave the Church. Over the years, I have watched, participated in, and designed evangelistic initiatives, hoping and praying the efforts would lead people to Jesus Christ. With great joy, we may celebrate those people who have come to the end of their lives with the saving knowledge of Jesus Christ resonating in their souls. We can also celebrate those who even today live for Christ as a result of God graciously working through those initiatives.

However, in more recent years it has become very clear the Church in the United States is in trouble. Something is wrong. Most of the difficulty is self-inflicted, as we have failed in some substantive measure to be faithful to the core purposes for our existence.

J.R. Tolkien wrote his classic *Lord of the Rings* trilogy to weave great truths through an adventure of good versus evil, sacrifice, war, loss, and victory. The Hobbit begins with Bilbo Baggins enjoying a quiet and peaceful existence in the beautiful and tranquil shire. The hobbits were peace-loving, simple people who lived close to the earth in an ordered society. What they did not know, was that deep in the mountain Mordor, evil was brewing. The peace they enjoyed would be challenged, and their world would be turned upside down, as evil moved stealthily to gain a position to strike. Bilbo would come to know violence and war. So too would his nephew Frodo.

*Introduction* xi

As the story progresses, the rise of evil increases. All that was dear and of value to good men and women and society, would be attacked through demon-like creatures. Frodo would have to enter into the thick of the battle against evil. So pervasive and poisonous was the evil, that Frodo would forever be tainted by his time as the ring bearer. The adventure would lead him to great battles, direct confrontation with evil, loss of friends, and his innocence.

The evil growing in our time mirrors that fictional story, but with one distinct difference—it is not fiction. Evil must be confronted, it is not to be appeased; ignoring it only makes it worse, evil must be confronted, and the future of society falls to the people of the Bible.

Some statistical data on church health in general in the United States reflects a downward trend. An article by Joshua Krish, "Americans Skeptical of God but Think Heaven Is Real, Somehow,"[1] states that since 1980, the number of those who believe in God has decreased by half.

> A San Diego State University study reported a current reality:
> 
> The percentage of Americans who prayed or believed in God reached an all-time low in 2014, according to new research led by San Diego State University psychology professor Jean M. Twenge.
> 
> A research team that included Ryne Sherman from Florida Atlantic University and Julie J. Exline and Joshua B. Grubbs from Case Western Reserve University analyzed data from 58,893 respondents to the General Social Survey, a nationally representative survey of U.S. adults administered between 1972 and 2014. Five times as many Americans in 2014 reported that they never prayed as did Americans in the early 1980s, and nearly twice as many said they did not believe in God.
> 
> Americans in recent years were less likely to engage in a wide variety of religious practices, including attending religious services, describing oneself as a religious person, and believing the Bible is divinely inspired, with the biggest declines seen among 18- to 29-year-old respondents. The results were published in the journal *Sage Open*.

"Most previous studies concluded that fewer Americans were publicly affiliating with a religion, but that Americans were just as religious in private ways. That's no longer the case, especially in the last few years," said Twenge, who is also the author of the book, *Generation Me*. "The large declines in religious practice among young adults are also further evidence that Millennials are the least religious generation in memory, and possibly in American history."

This decline in religious practice has not been accompanied by a rise in spirituality, which, according to Twenge, suggests that, rather than spirituality replacing religion, Americans are becoming more secular. The one exception to the decline in religious beliefs was a slight increase in belief in the afterlife.

"It was interesting that fewer people participated in religion or prayed but more believed in an afterlife," Twenge said. "It might be part of a growing entitlement mentality—thinking you can get something for nothing. There is a growing gap in the knowledge base and understanding of those who were born into and nurtured in the religion secularists, skepticism and disbelief. The degree to which Christian thought and influence is felt and esteemed in culture, is shrinking. The secular ideologues have patiently eroded the foundations, and disassembled the long-held traditions of the Christian Perhaps we have lost our way."[2]

While the Church slumbered through dramatic cultural shifts, a diabolical force took courage from our collective disarray, apathy, denominational and doctrinal silos, and began an all-out assault on the Church, its moral underpinnings, our Christian beliefs and practice, and the last vestiges of Christian influence in the public domain.

> *For our struggle is not against flesh and blood, but against the rulers, against the authorities, against the powers of this dark world and against the spiritual forces of evil in the heavenly realms (Ephesians 6:12).*

# Introduction

The source is not a new enemy, but an ancient foe, masked in both the soft cultural language of tolerance of deviant behavior, social "equality" for perversions over and above the freedom of religion, the debilitating philosophies of acquiescence, the assault on the Christian faith in academics, the law, media, and political correctness as a social poison masking as sensitivity. It is a sinister and evil ideology that uses predictable tactics. It diminishes accountability to anyone but one's self. It is a manifestation of a push for personal freedom with nothing to contain it and no constant against which right or wrong may be measured. It is the lack of any final basis against which vice and virtue are defined.

Centuries of fundamental assumptions within the preparation and practice of law have been strategically challenged. While early Western law had its roots in biblical and universally accepted truths, or natural law, those foundations were continually challenged and assaulted, and today, have given way. Such attacks manifest in the history revisionists who strive to marginalize the religious views and practices of those early settlers who fled religious intolerance, as my family did.

It manifests again in academic circles and in the halls of liberal institutions that seek to diminish the role of faith among our country's Founders, pervert their words and beliefs, and manufacture an alternative secular version palatable to the irreverent, godless desires of the poisoned and corrupt minds. It manifests in the loud vocal cries from segments of society who wish to shout down every form of traditional morality. It manifests in the evil, cruel, and violent actions of the extremely immoral as well as the bloodthirsty, radical Islamists who seek to overthrow the faith of others.

## Evil Aggression

In the late 1940s, a strategic assault began by those steeped in the belief that a separation between church and state meant the removal of references to Christian belief and practice in the public domain, with the justification being a fabrication and perversion of Thomas Jefferson's words, intent, and practice. The attack against expression of faith in the public domain continues with evil aggression, regardless of the cultural adoption of such beliefs as core to and characteristically part of the American experience.

So insidious is this evil that it manifests even within the Church, in the form of sects not motivated by the love and grace of God, but by a self-righteous corruption leading to flawed judgmentalism and a spirit of religion. That flaw twists and turns the Gospel message into something grotesque and ugly, rather than beautiful and redemptive. The Church, in her egregious weakness, has allowed the narrative and critique of Christian belief to erode the sure foundation of the biblical basis upon which morals, doctrine, and the redemptive message of a personal relationship with Jesus Christ is built. Whatever the combination of causes and variables might be, the source is evil.

The battle between good and evil rages. Sometimes we do not see the battle lines clearly. In the fog of battle, confusion becomes a tool of the enemy. He lies, distorts, plots, strategizes, and deceives. He employs every tactic necessary to win a victory. He will use our strengths, our weaknesses, our faults, and our virtues. He will play to our ego, our pride, and our vices. He will destroy our leaders, undermine our work, discourage our spirits, test our resolve, and create disunity.

But we are called to enter the fray. We are called to be part of the solution. We are called to be agents and ambassadors of redemption; and when necessary, enter the arena of a spiritual battle, manifesting, at times, in the flesh. We are called to rescue our fallen, and return them to the fold to fight another day. We never go in alone—we go with the Holy Spirit of God and with His power working through us. We are called not to a spirit of timidity but of boldness.

President Theodore Roosevelt, spoke the following remarks. They inspire us—men and women—to enter the arena, to give our all, to fight the good fight, to give ourselves to something that matters and lasts beyond the temporary inconsequential pursuits of this life.

> It is not the critic who counts; not the man who points out
> how the strong man stumbles, or where the doer of deeds

could have done them better. The credit belongs to the man who is actually in the arena, whose face is marred by dust and sweat and blood; who strives valiantly; who errs, who comes short again and again, because there is no effort without error and shortcoming; but who does strive to do the deeds; who knows great enthusiasms, the great devotions; who spends himself in a worthy cause; who at the best knows in the end the triumph of high achievement, and who at the worst, if he fails, at least fails while daring greatly, so his place shall never be with those cold and timid souls who neither know victory nor defeat. –Theodore Roosevelt, April 1910, from a speech in Paris, France, "Citizenship in a Republic"

Christian, Church, wake up and enter the arena!

## Consider…

*What point or points caught your attention as important and why?*

*What concept was new and requires additional time to process?*

*What action do you need to take as a result of what you read in this chapter?*

*What does the Holy Spirit say to you as you contemplate the chapter?*

*An increasingly secular society will attempt to redefine evil as any form of opposition to the values of the collective. Do you agree with this definition?*

Chapter 1

# Strategic, Targeted, Evangelistic Plans

Beyond the obvious reasons of a biblical mandate, a biblical history, a historical example, and a life impacting message, the local church needs effective **S**trategic, **T**argeted, **E**vangelistic **P**lans (STEP) steps toward moving God's Kingdom throughout the world. Many churches talk about evangelism, and may even engage in some form of effort to draw people to Jesus Christ. But many, it seems, have not yet homed in on their unique opportunities, combinations of qualities, giftedness, and points of passion that make their efforts successful. The STEP strategy was field tested, evaluated, and determined to help in developing effective evangelistic opportunities while at the same time creating a level of enthusiasm among participants.

As told in the biblical book of Acts, the early church experienced significant and rapid growth. The Holy Spirit moved freely through the church. Empowered by the Holy Spirit, committed to preaching the Gospel, willing to die for their mission, the Holy Spirit moved. Efforts, not guided or informed by the moving of the Holy Spirit, will have only normal results. The breath of God is needed and the ultimate context of His enabling power. This book outlines relevant points about the times and challenges to the Church and her mission of reconciling people to Jesus Christ. Also pointed out is the theological basis of the case for evangelism's preeminence as a role for the Church. After more than thirty years of an emphasis on building leaders in seminaries, churches, and parachurch organizations, little improvement has been made in culture. Churches close at record rates, social degradation continues at unprecedented levels, moral conduct falls to vile behavior. For all our focus, our redemptive influence has faltered. We must yield to the Holy Spirit who then guides our leaders, processes and mission efforts.

Given current trends in North America, specifically relating to projected church attendance decline, something must change in our collective approach to the subject of Kingdom growth. The STEP system provides a customized solution to the needs and possibilities within a local church. Prior to delving into the strategies, it is important to get an accurate picture of where we are today.

If you visit Amazon.com to look for a book on the subject of "spirituality," you will find a wide variety of religious viewpoints—and a limited Christian evangelical offering. Spirituality is popular. Celebrities with seemingly little or no connection to a Christian worldview, speak about their "spirituality." Many Americans track the lives and personal views of celebrities, athletes, political figures, and media personalities. As a result, culture moves, if only incrementally, toward views originating, in part, in the entertainment community and embraced by media outlets. The sports and entertainment community is an epicenter of cultural influence and a source of validation for those who share similar views with specific entertainment personalities.

To a greater extent, those who dominate a particular market segment tend to share common values and views to be accepted by the establishment. Hollywood, for instance, tends to be more ideologically liberal. Someone entering into that arena would be expected to embrace the overarching philosophy espoused by the power centers. Even a casual observer can determine that among evangelicals, the epicenters of media control influence our worldview. Add to that reality, an aggressive spin machine that works to create an ideological narrative that forces compliance, and even evangelicals succumb to the pressure.

Recent events in the political realm teach us significant lessons about the extent to which we as evangelicals move away from views we might have thought were firmly planted in our identity.

We often make decisions about our political leaders, in part, with an interest in their views on Christians and Christianity. In the 2016 Republican primary, the two front runners could not have been more different in how they wove the integration of a Christian worldview into the fabric of their candidacy. Both courted the evangelical vote. Ted Cruz is a preacher's kid. His language was rich in those traditional points that many evangelicals embrace and desire in a candidate. Donald Trump was less vocal about his faith, but assured the voters that he had some. Evangelicals were split, and the primary process eliminated the strong evangelical.

Some Christians had difficulty with "those other Christians" who liked Trump over what was favorable and "obviously spiritually" more desirable in Cruz. Can we with absolute confidence suggest that the Trump supporters were blind to the comparative gulf in spiritual acumen between the two and therefore "in the wrong" to have supported him? That question, and the sentiment that so dominated the passion and fervor on both sides, reveals something of far greater significance within the Church. To some extent, differing opinions as to a candidate's fitness for public office and the passions ignited in the electorate, reflects a far greater gulf within evangelical Christianity than we may be comfortable admitting. So diverse are the various nuances of belief, attitude, expectation, and practice within that it almost seems absurd to expect that well-meaning believers can consistently move as a voting block on all issues.

## Wading in the Weeds

There exists among some within the household of faith, the belief that all who profess Christ share a set of values, attitudes, dispositions, and morals that transcend the "lesser" issues. Such thinking betrays a penchant for seeking easy answers and a reluctance to wade in the weeds of the collective cultural disposition among evangelicals, and the extent to which cultural influence integrates the lives of all people. Our failure to grasp that point is to our shame. It may signify an inability to accurately assess the great diversity of belief and practice within the community of faith.

Are there values, attitudes, and beliefs that are substantive enough to be the only lens among evangelicals through which all ideas and issues are filtered? Some would respond with a passionate assertion that such should be the case. If that is so, and the results of a polarizing election polarized even the evangelicals, it should be clear that a gap exists internally between what we should reasonably expect, and what is.

Is it possible to move a mission forward when the great disparity as to the nature, purpose, and rationale for the mission in and of itself creates pockets of dissimilar practice? No effective movement can move forward when it is based on and held together by points in which we differ. We can only move forward based on points we hold in common. It would appear that what we hold in common is less than we expected. The fabrics of similar cloth are held together, if held together at all, by weak strands that do not fit, bond, or unite. Our fabric of unity is built on our emphasis of our denominational color, not the scarlet thread that is the true piece at the core of our identity.

It then becomes necessary to define the points evangelicals can hold in common. What does indeed form the consistent and deeply held immutable truths that knit us together? What common belief will enable us to develop a position of strength and unity from which we strategically introduce Christ? Should we even care?

If we look beyond the surface of the traditional news sources, we will detect an increasingly hostile pattern of behavior directed at the Church, while other spiritual options gain acceptance. At this point in history, the increase of the Islam religion in the world community after 9-11, coupled with an increased boldness and casual acceptance of alternative practices, and the open and bold assault from Satanists in main stream venues, points to a strong cultural decline in Christian influence as a mitigating presence in society.

Worse yet, church attendance continues to shrink. As Wolfgang Simson suggests, the current attitude among the general populace toward the Church is, "God yes, church no."[1] Spirituality is popular in the culture today, and many citizens are looking for a connection with something other than what churches have to offer. Our internal measures, focus, strategies, decision making processes, and budgetary concerns do not adequately address the problem of decline. Nor do we wade into the underbelly of need among the disadvantaged, the abused, the suffering, all of which occurs under our noses and to a degree that should sicken us. Human trafficking, abuse of children, exploitation of women held in captivity in sex trades—the work before us is massive, and too many are at play in the inner sanctum of their church walls. Rise up, Christians!

Every age faces particular problems in communicating and gaining social influence in the mission of Kingdom expansion. If not addressed, the problems may result in a myriad of negative consequences for culture collectively, and individuals more specifically. The negative consequences of a cultural collapse lacking in Christian influence will have both short-term and long-term consequences. The consequences will certainly be inconsistent with the nature of our mission and counter to our beliefs. This is true not only in the sense that fewer people come to a saving knowledge of Jesus Christ, but also good Christian values and norms may receive punitive actions from secularists. To advance the reassertion of Christian values in a rapidly changing world, five points of focused attention is required:

1. Strategic Thinking
2. Global Action
3. Epicenters of Cultural Influence
4. Excellence in Execution
5. Multitude of Disciplines

We live in a time when, ironically, there is an emphasis on leadership within the church, but competencies, skill sets, and abilities are seemingly inadequate and cannot keep pace with the need or the speed of cultural changes into which a message is to be taken. There are leadership seminars everywhere within the faith community. Seminaries and other Christian institutions offer degrees with leadership focus. Many continuing educational programs and denominational training also emphasize leadership development.

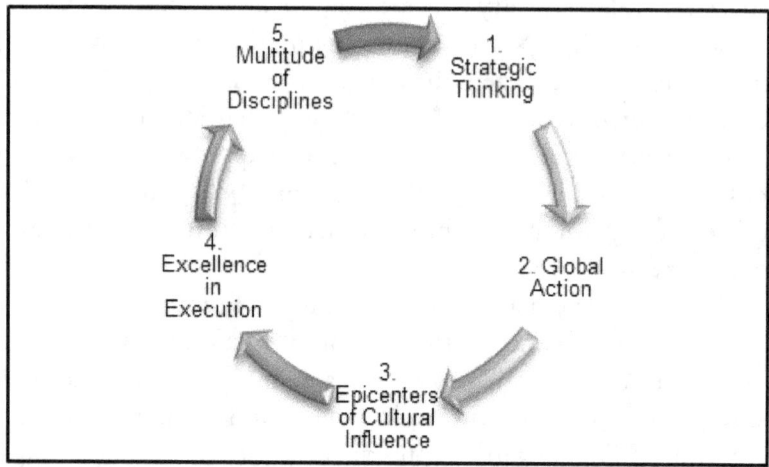

However, the need for leadership continues to grow and morph due, in part, to rapid cultural shifts. Couple that reality with a sonic pace of technological change, a disposition of cultural and religious pluralism, generational changes, economic globalization, and social contact tools and trends. Those factors, among others, contribute to an increased clash of domestic cultural ideologies and precipitous degradation of social mores ordinarily associated with Christian values. Other ideas flood the marketplace of human interaction.

Some historical Christian values, believed to be so much a part of the American culture, are waning. There exists a degree of disbelief among the faithful. Churches in the United States is waking up to the reality that their influence in culture is nearly gone. As we begin to wipe the sleep from our eyes and mutter, "It cannot be!" the denial contributes to the paralysis in addressing the obvious decline.

In some instances, we have watched the dramatic erosion of Christian values once thought firmly established and imbedded in the fabric of American culture. Other countries, like Great Britain, France, and Germany, have already experienced such declines, and have witnessed the ascension of ideologies inconsistent with their own historical and commonly held Christian values, and both the churches and the culture have suffered for it. Other ideologies have moved into the epicenters of cultural influence. As a result, the Europe of today is not the Europe of even fifty years ago.

Each country now faces challenges to long-held traditions and values, under the banner of inclusion, tolerance, and in some countries, a frontal usurpation of law. Those countries serve as harbingers of the possibility for any culture that fails to effectively tend to the core of the Christian mission.

We will further examine typical evangelistic approaches and potential problems connected to using them exclusively in the diverse American culture. A STEP systematic framework in the local church will curb the current low rates of national church growth.

The American culture is segmented into groups based on economic position, ethnicity, educational level, common bonds, social position, interest, cultural and social considerations, and a whole host of additional variables. Some of the points of connection are difficult to discern, understand, and in some cases, gather information. The ability of the local church to communicate the gospel effectively is proportional to its ability to speak the "language" of those diverse groups.

A "one size fits all" approach to evangelism will not yield the desired results. There will be multitudes of people who will not come to faith in Jesus Christ, because the church has been less than diligent and engaged at the necessary level. The STEP system exists as a tool with which we may reverse the trend. The STEP system catalogs the major evangelistic approaches that may be employed within the local church or ministry setting, and then develops an integrative, customized structure. The design takes into consideration the unique qualities of the specific target groups, the giftedness and attributes of a local congregation or body of believers.

The STEP design increases the effectiveness of the local church or group of believers in evangelistic efforts by understanding the realities of the current society, immediate context, and the various options available. STEP guides a congregation or ministry to identify specific potential evangelistic opportunities, determine best methods for effectively reaching them, establish workable team approaches, set timelines, and rank priorities according to the bottom line of new disciples.

The analysis of the process includes evangelistic efforts already in progress, as well as initiatives arising out of the STEP system. The ultimate measure of system success is the number of conversions, participation of group members, individual attitudes toward evangelistic efforts after involvement, and sustainability for continued ministry impact.

The system does not address the follow-up of discipleship and equipping. It does not spell out all of the options. Rather, it provides a framework to help participants discover and customize opportunities they can then execute. STEP deals primarily with strategic outreach planning, and mechanisms for improving effectiveness.

Analysis of modern-day statistics confirms the need for and viability of the STEP system—a customizable system that results in conversions and a greater enthusiasm among participants, achieving primary objectives.

## Significant Challenges

Additional factors exist that pose significant challenges to the Church. We face issues relevant to an aging population, transfer of wealth from one generation to another, and lifestyle values in conflict with those cultural shifts. For Christians, the problems increase by trends toward secularization of the Christian faith, encroachment from other belief systems, and disagreements in our own ranks as to the shape, structure, and practice of Christian life. While some shifts benefit the church and help to connect with others, there are significant dangers with associated with secularization. Each of the trends reflected in the following graph pose significant problems for the Church, but nothing that is insurmountable.

It seems the Christian community is allowing others to define and frame the issues, as well as determine for us the operative context and practice of our own faith. Some would argue the trend is irreversible. We naturally disagree with those pronouncements. The points here are: 1) God is Sovereign; 2) He commands an evangelistic role for the Church; 3) The Church grew out of a minority status, in spite of opposition from dominant beliefs and ideologies; 5) Turning the tide is dependent on a few willing to commit themselves to the core functions of the Church. The latter issue brings into question the level of leadership within the Church.[2]

Table 2.
Population by Race and Hispanic Origin: 2014 and 2060
(Population in thousands)

| Race and Hispanic origin[1] | 2014 | | 2060 | | Change, 2014 to 2060 | |
|---|---|---|---|---|---|---|
| | Number | Percent | Number | Percent | Number | Percent |
| Total population | 318,748 | 100.0 | 416,795 | 100.0 | 98,047 | 30.8 |
| One Race | 310,753 | 97.5 | 390,772 | 93.8 | 80,020 | 25.8 |
| White | 246,940 | 77.5 | 285,314 | 68.5 | 38,374 | 15.5 |
| Non-Hispanic White | 198,103 | 62.2 | 181,930 | 43.6 | −16,174 | −8.2 |
| Black or African American | 42,039 | 13.2 | 59,693 | 14.3 | 17,654 | 42.0 |
| American Indian and Alaska Native | 3,957 | 1.2 | 5,607 | 1.3 | 1,650 | 41.7 |
| Asian | 17,083 | 5.4 | 38,965 | 9.3 | 21,882 | 128.1 |
| Native Hawaiian and Other Pacific Islander | 734 | 0.2 | 1,194 | 0.3 | 460 | 62.6 |
| Two or More Races | 7,995 | 2.5 | 26,022 | 6.2 | 18,027 | 225.5 |
| Race Alone or in Combination[3] | | | | | | |
| White | 254,009 | 79.7 | 309,567 | 74.3 | 55,558 | 21.9 |
| Black or African American | 45,562 | 14.3 | 74,530 | 17.9 | 28,968 | 63.6 |
| American Indian and Alaska Native | 6,528 | 2.0 | 10,169 | 2.4 | 3,640 | 55.8 |
| Asian | 19,983 | 6.3 | 48,575 | 11.7 | 28,592 | 143.1 |
| Native Hawaiian and Other Pacific Islander | 1,458 | 0.5 | 2,929 | 0.7 | 1,470 | 100.8 |
| Hispanic or Latino Origin | | | | | | |
| Hispanic | 55,410 | 17.4 | 119,044 | 28.6 | 63,635 | 114.8 |
| Not Hispanic | 263,338 | 82.6 | 297,750 | 71.4 | 34,412 | 13.1 |

[1] Hispanic origin is considered an ethnicity, not a race. Hispanics may be of any race. Responses of "Some Other Race" from the 2010 Census are modified. For more information, see <www.census.gov/popest/data/historical/files/MRSF-01-US1.pdf>.
[2] "In combination" means in combination with one or more other races. The sum of the five race groups adds to more than the total population, and 100 percent, because individuals may report more than one race.
Source: U.S. Census Bureau, 2014 National Projections.

The local church faces a leadership crisis. The traditional educational outlets designed to build and prepare effective leaders for the Church hinder development of market-driven opportunities in leadership advancement due to rigid adherence to antiquated procedures, institutional barriers, and organizational impediments In short, we are not structured to meet the need. Some of the guiding coalitions in pastoral training and development continue with structures, systems, and presupposition, no longer holding any connection to cataclysmic cultural shifts. Despite the focus on developing leaders, principally among the practitioners, we still see decline in our country. Cultural shifts toward godlessness at the epicenters of social control, point to that failure.

Acquiescence to federal mandates, educational structures, operational procedures, dependence on federal dollars, and an inadequate grasp of reality within some Christian accreditation bodies, create an environment driven not by missional decision making at its finest, but an overt and covert usurpation. The result is unresponsive, slow, or ineffective systems that lag behind the innovation curve of changing cultural realities. As a result, Christian influence within society declines as a whole. The collective force of the cumulative impact upon culture from a Christian point of view, and those traditionally tasked with advancing it, is dwindling.

## The Point of the Spear

The point of the spear is the preparation of those who will lead on the front lines: the pastors of local churches and ministries and those among them who will become active players in the great commission adventure. The apparent inability to motivate disciples within the local church into passionate mission-focused people, points to the preparatory processes being out of step with the need. Combine that with the relatively short tenure of ministry leaders, and it is easy to see that local churches are in perilous leadership times.

Culture has so radically changed, and our systems so lagging behind that our message gives the appearance to young and old eyes alike of being irrelevant, out of touch, and of little consequence. Many years too late, we are only now beginning to realize the extent to which that is true. Too many churches have not confronted the ugly truths of not only a lack of evangelistic effectiveness, but the cultural shift in which we now exist. We still do not comprehend the collective cultural intolerance toward Christians—from the "tolerance crowd."

Those who do see and understand the precipitous decline, at times adjust strategy enough to communicate a public awareness of being out of touch, and over-correct to get back in touch. The result on some occasions begins to look like fruitless pandering, not culturally redemptive leadership. For our part, Christians, with our Sunday morning worship wars, "Tea Party" parishioners (who show greater concern for national issues over Kingdom and spiritual issues), a few self-righteous television preachers, whining and warning blog spots, and inconsistent living among our numbers, make us easy targets. The Church is portrayed as collections of ignorant, unsophisticated people, out of touch with reality, and brandishing a fairy tale through which we add meaningless significance to our lives—and rob everyone else of their pursuit of happiness.

We sometimes aid and abet that egregiously wrong characterization by becoming a parody of ourselves. We further exacerbate the problem by failing to define the narrative. Instead, we cede the narrative of ourselves and our faith to those outside the Church who are simply hostile to its existence, and inside the faith by those wishing to moderate the exclusive distinctive as they contrast with other religions. There are those who resist the biblical and historical, exclusionary claims of Christ. The view of the Church by both groups, is a grand collection of unsavory and problematic nuisances in an otherwise healthy culture. We are, simply, mere hypocrites.

Enter Pope Frances, whose liberation theology soaks each doctrinal position with an abridged level of tolerance for behaviors out of step with long-held orthodoxy, attacks on the economic foundation of free enterprise systems, with a corresponding attempt to use his influence to promote a redistribution ideology, fostering a form of "social justice," which is just for the wage earner and penalizes and rebukes the wage payer. It is social justice in name only, not in application, nor appropriate for all economic systems. It is tantamount to a misdiagnosis with the administering of a lethal dose of a drug that negatively interacts with the host. It is the equivalent of cutting off the neck of the goose that lays the golden egg. He posits positions without the understanding of the long-term consequences and the harmful unintended results for the very people he wants to help.

In some cases, true justice is diminished, and a mask for a greater pathway of subservience to a governing authority is provided. All of which signal a further erosion from the largest Christian platform in the world. One leader, whose good heart and intentions are vested in fundamentally flawed ideology, wrapped in Christian verbiage, skews the norms of biblical acceptability. While the current pope's liberation theology seeks to free the masses from social and economic injustice, it enslaves them to an ideology that diminishes freedom and opportunity. The people lose in the exchange.

Of great concern is the acquiescence or over-correction to culture, over and above the adherence to sound biblical doctrine that has been engrained in the body of believers since the time of Christ. Several mainline denominations have determined that what was wrong is now right, and the way to bring in people is to allow behavior not consistent with historical Christianity. The ordination of homosexuals, the marriage of homosexuals, the acceptance of godless sexual deviance, is embraced as a means by which we show "love" for the lost. The admonitions of Christ are no longer the defining measure of what constitutes a disciple of Christ.

Rather, evil conduct, where everyone does what they see as right in their own eyes, are the accepted and promoted measures. Of greater value to them than the Scriptures is the changing flavor of accepted practices within culture. Culture, then, becomes the arbiter of right and wrong, and it is wrong to bring the Scriptures to bear upon culture. Such a reality is a manifestation of evil. It is as John Coffee, the character in *The Green Mile* movie, proclaimed, "He killed them with they love."

It is time for the Church to take another tact. We are, in every sense of the word and in every possible form, sinners, saved by the phenomenal grace of God, lovingly extended to everyone who has confessed their unworthiness and gross imperfections before a perfect God, and received the undeserved forgiveness of God through the once-for-all sacrifice of Jesus Christ. That the public and other voices in society do not understand that truth is our fault, not theirs. It is a reflection of our ineffectiveness and, in some cases, down-right laziness. It is a failure to point to and focus on the perfection of and sufficiency in Christ, rather than anything based on our own merit.

## It is a Trap

No matter how holy, self-disciplined, and righteous we try to appear, it is never enough. It comes off as arrogant sanctimony. That poison courses violently through the Church, and is a form of deeply rooted self-deception—the very thing that feeds the beast of opposition to the Church. With every charge pointed against the obvious flaws of those within the Church, we recoil and try harder to reach perfection by modifying our behavior so we meet the expectations of those who cry, "Hypocrite." But it is a trap.

Rather, we should simply acknowledge our imperfections. We are human. Then point to the flawless perfection of Christ and the grace extended by faith in Him, despite our worst selves. We point to our complete dependence on Him. What ultimately distinguishes us from others, is the character and nature of the One in whom we place our faith as the remedy for our fallen nature and as the basis of reconciliation with God. Our individual and collective flaws are lifetime struggles. We work out those struggles, whatever they may be, on this side of life, in the context of life lived out before everyone.

Perfection alludes us. But it did not allude Christ. Our flaws are too pronounced to pretend they do not still exist. Far better to acknowledge our sinfulness openly, and point to the Ultimate Remedy for our condition, than try to create a façade that we have reached a state of perfection through our own, personal agency.

Rather than acquiesce to a corrupt narrative and other similar notions, our focus, energy, and effort are directed to actions that provide the potential for greatest impact in the shortest period, with the likelihood of longer term success and sustained advancement.

## The Goal

The goal, therefore, is to develop, customize, implement, and integrate, strategic and targeted evangelistic plans—STEPs—for the local church that are effective in reaching a variety of individuals within subcultures or affinity groups to advance, expand, the Kingdom of God.

The degree to which strategic approaches are successful depend, in large part, on the leadership brought to bear on the initiative and the responsiveness of the participants. Participants must prepare, and prepare well. Aggressive equipping and discipleship, with a high degree of spiritual maturity, is necessary for success. It is not a "Come one, come all" approach. It will require traits and characteristics in participants, not found in the whole of the congregation or group. In fact, those traits and characteristics may not be found at all within a church. That means the church will limp along until it dies or is revived, and the Holy Spirit of God begins to move.

A few words and definitions:

- *Strategy:* A careful plan or method for achieving a particular goal, usually over a long period of time.
- *Church:* The collection of souls of those professing Jesus Christ as Savior in all its diversity of doctrines, denominations, languages, and personalities.
- *Audience:* The specific people or persons, groups of people, or segments of society who are identified for evangelistic outreach.

A strategic evangelistic approach:

1. Makes use of the best possible methods for the specific group. It is also strategic when those approaches are based on solid intelligence, pertinent information relative to the audience.
2. Ensures an integrative approach, which means possessing a willingness to use any combination of strategies and tools at any given time for specific audience, to achieve optimal effectiveness.
3. Maintains a high degree of adaptability to the audience to be reached, with consideration for their interests, sensitivities, desires, and behavioral preferences, which therefore dictates the methods integrated into the strategy.
4. Builds awareness and sensitivity within the church, relative to the reality of diversity. It shapes evangelistic strategies to reach the unique groups.
5. Accumulates a working knowledge of an audience background, tastes, interest, priorities, intelligence and experience, which aids in bringing about evangelistic victories.

When we ignore the reality of continuing growth in ethnic and cultural diversity, we move closer to being ineffective rather than effective, in terms of our outreach as the Church.

Evangelistic outreach, in the way it occurs in many churches today, is not the integration of strategic planning into the fabric of the life of the church, or of the church into the myriad of sub-cultural opportunities. Many churches gravitate to simple, time-honored methods of evangelism that have less and less impact on conversion rates. Across much of the country, techniques and strategies tend to be adopted as they are found in the Christian consumer marketplace.

As the cultural and ethnic make-up continues to change—the significant cultural diversity, subcultures, and the multiple layers of the social onion—packaged programs may not keep pace. Keeping on top of and specifically targeting people groups to reach, with standard operating procedures, may not bring about the results and impact that a concerted, customized strategy can bring. There may be some degree to which our existing publishing houses, which develop concepts and curricula for application in the local church, by way of unintended consequence, limit the scope and reach of local churches and ministries. There is a better way.

Our diversity as a nation is an opportunity for the Church. The country is not a monolithic collection of homogeneous citizens. It is, instead, a hugely diversified populace with a wide variety of ethnic groups, interests, likes, dislikes, behavioral patterns, purchasing preferences, religious interests, etc. The American culture is a collection of subcultures and interest groups, each with characteristics and traits unique to them. That fact has significant implications for society and churches in particular.

Census projections indicate an increasingly ethnic diversity through 2060. Some ethnicities are anticipated to increase as much as 225 percent by 2060. "Non-Hispanic white" is the only group that sees a decline. All other ethnic groups will enjoy steady increases. Those changing factors, as well as the cultural nuances of each, represent a significant challenge for churches and Christian ministries in the USA. We may celebrate the melting pot diversity, while at the same time recognizing that the methodologies of outreach must shift.

Natan Sharansky writes in his book, The Case for Democracy:

Human diversity suggests that change within any society is inevitable. No two people, much less all the members of a community, have the same background, tastes, interests, priorities, curiosity, intelligence, and experiences. These natural differences will invariably lead people to respond to new situations in different ways. No matter how homogeneous a society may seem, eventually differences will emerge and grow. The speed with which this process occurs will depend on many factors, from how large and complex the society is to the degree of its exposure to outside influences, but differences of opinions are certain. The question then becomes how the hypothetical society will respond to these inevitable differences in opinion.[3]

By way of illustration, consider the depth of diversity in American culture through T-shirts. The online T-Shirt industry is enjoying a robust expansion. *Ibis World* reports a record $68 million in revenue, just from online sources in 2014.[4] They are enjoying a 24 percent annual increase in sales. Brick and mortar stores will increase. Americans purchase and literally wear their interests on their sleeve, and each shirt has something that reflects a connection to or affinity for some subculture group, interest or ideology with which they identify. There is often a language, attitude, symbolism, nomenclature, and even culture associated with each group represented on a printed shirt. Donald N. Thompson, in his book *Oracles,* writes that "Google is a T-shirt economy; people will volunteer for all sorts of things and do work for other teams just to get a cool T-shirt."[5]

Clues to a person's interest are all over. From clothing to cars, we often advertise what holds some value for us. Facebook allows individuals to announce to the public points of personal interest and the things that mean the most to them. They can post who they like, what they do, how they spend their time, the conversations they have, where they like to go, who they like to associate with, what they like and dislike, their philosophical, religious and political views. Facebook makes people relative open books to the public at large. Pinterest does much the same thing. Those two commonplace social media tools are open windows into an individual or a group. Both tools help us as social creatures remain connected to the larger community of friends, family, work, sports, and leisure. Today, very little Holmesian deductive art is needed to gather information, thanks to the Internet.

When we consider the wide array of hobbies, occupations, pastimes, and interests—it is reasonable to conclude that each person or group represents an opportunity for the church to connect. What Sharansky states as true of society in general is true of the church in society as well. How the church responds to the inevitable differences in culture is determining the level of influence in society as a whole.

## Consider...

*What point or points caught your attention as important and why?*

*What concept was new and requires additional time to process?*

*What action do you need to take as a result of what you read in this chapter?*

*What does the Holy Spirit say to you as you contemplate the chapter?*

*"Of greater value to them than the Scriptures is the changing flavor of accepted practices within culture. Culture, then, becomes the arbiter of right and wrong, and it is wrong to bring the Scriptures to bear upon culture."* Do you agree with this summation? Have you witnessed this reality within your own social community?

CHAPTER 2

# Societal and Cultural Battlefields

It is a strategic imperative that the Church bring Kingdom increase by sending forces into the arena of the societal battlefield, rather than focusing on strategies dependent on attracting to the church. While there is validity to the default strategy, it decreases the biblical mandate of sending.

Leslie Newbigin writes, "If the gospel is to be understood, if it is to be received as something that communicates truth about the real human condition, if it is, as we say, to 'make sense,' it has to be communicated in the language of those to whom it is addressed and has to be clothed in symbols which are meaningful to them."[1] Newbigin poses a significant challenge to the way some evangelistic efforts are conducted. To communicate in the language of an interest group or subculture, we need to speak their language. The strategic and integrative approach to evangelism can move an organization to determine the extent to which that is possible for them.

The Church seems to lag behind significantly in its ability to read, adapt to, understand the implications of, and communicate its message in an ever-changing culture. In a time when the door has swung wide open for us to meet new people, reconnect with old friends, and engage on friendly turf, not much relative strategy has been developed. It seems that believers openly state their views, but do not necessarily choose wisely in how they engage others who may not share their view. There is a price paid in souls for not being wise enough to understand the times and proactively plan and strategize accordingly.

Many local churches and ministries are largely ineffective at penetrating subcultures with the gospel. Some do not have the shrewdness, resolve, or the drive to do whatever it takes to reach various subcultures and interest groups for Christ. To do so, in a strategic and integrative fashion, represents a significant shift in the way many churches function and the amount of time and energy a local body invests in such an endeavor. Yet, apart from being a worshiping community, outreach and evangelism is our core mission.

There is no evangelistic approach that is effective every time and in every situation. Yet many churches continue to use models of evangelism from bygone eras or focus on service provision and soft contact and then wonder why there is so little impact in society. Service is a visible and socially impactful strategy. However, there must be a subsequent effort that begins to "draw the net" through conversion. Fishers of men and women catch fish. The church that understands culture, adapts strategies to it, and constantly improves to meet the ever-changing social challenges will be more successful in living out their core mission.

## The Cheese Keeps Moving

The cheese keeps moving, and the Church needs to adapt to change, change quickly, enjoy the change, be ready to change quickly and enjoy it repeatedly to affect culture. Jesus was a master of culture. He would readily adapt His approach and say just the right thing at just the right time.[2] He knew the way people thought and responded accordingly. His example is that of taking every opportunity, using common, everyday issues of importance, and bending the conversation or presentation to fit the current need.

Advancing Kingdom work is the core function of the believer and the measure of measures. The means by which we achieve the objectives varies, in part, by vocation. The Church as a whole needs a comprehensive, Christian shift, by which it, and those who are part of the Church, gain an appropriate level of commitment to their call as believers. That shift begins with the leader.

Some suggest the traditional church is no longer the vessel for effective outreach. Antiquated ideas, lack of understanding about shifts and trends in culture and associated behavioral patterns, power struggles, preconceived notions about the culture, internal struggles, fear of change, lack of innovation, short-term event-driven efforts, and a failure to strategically plan all contribute to marginal evangelistic effectiveness in many churches today. It takes Christian leaders to move the mission forward, and a committed body of believers to move alongside them.

It seems as if many churches are not willing to do the hard, strategic work needed to gain all the information necessary to target specific segments, and thereby ensure evangelistic effectiveness. Far too often, simply choosing a tried and true method of a bygone era is the preferred option of choice.

## Apathy Prevails

Apathy among church attendees is also a considerable problem. For example, one denominational congregation informed their ecclesiastical conference that they had no interest in growing in their ministry context. At least that group was honest about their lack of concern for effective outreach. Others only give lip service to it. People gravitate to the known. Not many people are innovators. The Church as a whole pays a price because of that reality.

Dr. Howard Foltz wrote in his book, *Healthy Churches in a Sick World*:

> Perhaps our churches are missing the mark because we aren't even aiming at the target. In essence, our churches have become cultural cocoons where people believe their main function is to sit and fellowship with the back of somebody else's head. Largely, believers have adopted an attitude that says the church exists to meet their needs rather than the worlds. Of course, the church does exist to help God meet the congregation's needs, but ministry cannot stop there.[3]

His view captures well the malaise that characterizes the Church in North America. We are not all in alignment with the values and purposes God has called us to fulfill. Something has to change. While some may view the Church as bordering on consumerism, there is validity in aiming the gospel at consumers and borrowing from effective, proven disciplines and cultural connecting points. To hit the target, the aim has to be right on. If critical information about the target can help sharpen the focus and increase the likelihood of striking it, that is valid. Leaders and churches have to adopt greater, more effective strategies that capitalize on current cultural realities, rather than deny them.

The STEP system is a methodology based on the assumption that any given approach, determined by accurate research and effective implementation, would most likely increase the quantity of people brought to Jesus Christ through the ministry of the local church or para-church organization.

## Strategic Outreach Efforts

Writing this book arose out of the consuming conviction that churches have an outreach orientation. Alignment with the purposes of God yields great results. When we are out of alignment, we do not function as intended. With the proper tools and a solid framework for planning, implementing, and evaluating evangelistic efforts, some churches could dramatically improve their impact on the lives of many people. Those efforts must not be token, half-hearted attempts to make a difference. Rather, churches must once again become evangelistic power houses that challenge every segment of the culture through an effective message.

When only a modicum of concern exists within the life of any given group of believers, a leader must reevaluate their time and commitment. If God has called them to that particular location, one cannot argue against it. However, if the passion of that calling is for a greater aggressiveness evangelistically, the fit must considered.

Strategic outreach efforts will result in an increase of people worshiping and living for Christ through the ministry. There are people within the reach of most churches. Effective strategies of communicating transformational truth will change them. We must ask, why is it not happening now? Conversion rates are low overall and flat in some churches. Why are so many conversion rates low? There are internal, often times strategic, failings that contribute to the lack of effectiveness. To experience positive conversion growth within the Church, the local church must become strategic in its evangelistic efforts, and culturally perceptive.

## Why?

Many mainline denominations within the United States have experienced stagnation or decline. Conversion growth fails to keep pace with the population and continues to lose ground.[4] Aubrey Malphurs writes that at the end of the last century, 80 to 85 percent of North American churches are either plateaued or in decline.[5]

While many churches recognize the need for evangelism, the organizational focus has been elsewhere, and evangelistic efforts have suffered as a result. It seems as if organizational values other than evangelism receive a greater share of resources, energy, and attention. If local church evangelism is done at all, it is often left to those few people who have the gift, or it is attempted using irrelevant and outdated methods that are ineffective in the postmodern culture.

Outdated methods, faulty assumptions, and myopic thinking contribute to failure. Of the growth that does occur, much of it is transfer growth. If the Church is to be faithful to the desires of Jesus Christ, it must reassert its collective energies and resources to accomplish the task.

Mark Mittelberg writes, "We need more than enthusiastic and equipped individuals. We also need the synergy of biblically functioning, outwardly focused, evangelistically active churches—and we need lots of them. We need churches to proactively partner with their members to reach increasing numbers of people who are far from God."[6]

## Biblical Perspectives

Throughout this book we will examine the various biblical and theological issues related to the need for conversion growth in the local church, discussing the Scriptures that form an understanding of the place and priority evangelism is to take in the local church. We cannot even begin to speak about strategy and integration of methodologies until we establish evangelism as necessary for the Church. It seems ludicrous to have to establish such an understanding, but successful efforts are rare in the cumulative. It is increasingly clear that leaders are critical for the success of evangelistic efforts, whatever they may be. However, there is an extent to which the competencies and skills, beyond spiritual giftedness, of even our best leaders need additional preparation for the cultural realities we face.

We need Christian leaders. A pastor or ministry leader will have a difficult time moving people to embrace culture strategically, if his or her leadership is questioned or resisted from the beginning. The presuppositions held by the laity in many churches across the country are in conflict with those in pastoral leadership. The role of the pastor is such that they should never acquiesce to a lesser notion of faith in practice, and the central core missions of the church. Rather, their role is to define for those with whom they have charge, the parameters of the mission, and not the other way around. Of course certain communities lend themselves to confusion on that issue, but pastors and leaders should have no confusion, and commit themselves to the high calling to which they have submitted.

There is a need for a two-part apologetic to set the foundation for effective cultural penetration. First, the biblical mandate to reach the lost needs to be established; second, the biblical role of the leader needs to be examined and accepted. Otherwise, strategies and methodologies succumb to efforts that thwart and undermine from within. Matthew 28:19-20 provides the foundational support.

The local church is to be an instrument through which the saving knowledge of Jesus Christ is spread to others outside the church. It has a responsibility to fulfill the Great Commission of Jesus Christ (Matthew 28). That responsibility is not to be taken lightly or dismissed. It is a necessary function of the local church. We, therefore, embrace and act upon with vigor, energy, and great commitment a great commission movement. It is through the faithful witness of the followers of Christ, the priesthood of believers, along with the proclamation of the gospel, that the church grows.

The following section considers Old and New Testament themes specifically related to evangelism, including:
- principles derived from those themes
- the paradigm formed by the biblical example
- support given for the position from theologians and Christian authors
- and how the local church is to respond to the wide range of support for the evangelistic efforts.

The combined weight of the commands of Jesus Christ, the example of the apostles, and the practice of the New Testament church and tradition all help to establish the legitimacy of the paradigm. There is sufficient evidence in both Old and New Testaments to conclude that evangelistic efforts are key functions of the followers of Christ.

## Old Testament Perspectives

Evangelism in the New Testament has its roots in the revelation of God to humanity in the Pentateuch, the historical books, wisdom and poetry, and the work of the prophets of the Old Testament. The *Oxford Companion to the Bible* states, "In the Hebrew bible we find the similar figure in the messenger who brings good news and proclaims peace." In the Pentateuch, God communicated to Moses at Horeb and divulged His intentions to deliver the Israelites from Egyptian bondage. That news was, in turn, communicated to pharaoh and to the Israelites in captivity. The Ten Commandments given to Moses guided the social conduct of the people and assured the worship of God.

God communicated as well through dreams, visions, and theophanies. Some of those were messages passed on to others, which took the form of rebukes, encouragement, judgment, or calls to repentance. In the historical books, God communicated His plans, promises, and general information that would aid His children in the lives they were leading. Gordon Lewis and Bruce Demarest point to the contest between Elijah and the prophets of Baal in 1 Kings 18:16-39 as a significant event that caused the onlookers to acknowledge Gods superiority.[7] They write, "God's specially revealed precepts and ordinances effect spiritual revitalization in the believer, impart spiritual understanding, give peace to troubled consciences, and implant the hope of final salvation."[8]

God gave His message to the prophets who communicated the Word and will of God. The prophetic message was often one of repentance and a call upon a people to turn back to God individually and as nations. Isaiah was given a message to speak to the people. He received his commission after having a vision of the Lord and becoming aware of the contrast between God's perfection and his own sinfulness. The realization of what God had done for him stirred Isaiah to respond to the Lord's call for service.

> *"Woe to me!" I cried. "I am ruined! For I am a man of unclean lips, and I live among a people of unclean lips, and my eyes have seen the King, the LORD Almighty." Then one of the seraphs flew to me with a live coal in his hand, which he had taken with tongs from the altar. With it he touched my mouth and said, "See, this has touched your lips; your guilt is taken away and your sin atoned for." Then I heard the voice of the Lord saying, "Whom shall I send? And who will go for us?" And I said, "Here am I. Send me!" He said, "Go and tell this people…" (Isaiah 6:5-9).*

All through the Old Testament God was revealing Himself to humanity and providing them the means by which they could live in His favor. The nature of the message changed in the New Testament, as people were called to serve Christ and advance the saving grace. In the Old Testament, God made provision for the salvation of pagan peoples by encouraging them to repent and recognize their need to obey and worship the one true God. The principle means of communication was through the prophetic role. There is significant difference between the two approaches. One difference is the understanding that an important role of the Church and the individual believer is to convey the good news of Christ and His atoning sacrifice on the cross.

## New Testament Perspectives

No other passage in Scripture provides a clearer and more complete picture of the mission Jesus gave to His followers than the Matthew 28 passage. At the close of His life, Jesus addressed the future mission, purpose, and ministry of His followers from that time forward. His instructions were clear, concise, and based on the authority and power that is His. The Great Commission of Jesus Christ stands as the marching order for all churches in all parts of the world for all time until His return: *"Therefore go and make disciples of all nations, baptizing them in the name of the Father and of the Son and of the Holy Spirit, and teaching them to obey everything I have commanded you. And surely I am with you always, to the very end of the age"* (Matthew 28:19-20).

The verb form of "make disciples" (metheteusate) is expressed in the imperative: "From the perspective of mission strategy, it is important to remember that Great Commission is preserved in several complementary forms that taken together can only be circumvented by considerable exegetical ingenuity."[9]

The command is binding for all the followers of Christ. They must be committed enough to act on the desires of Christ to bring others into the grace that they themselves have found in Christ Jesus. So strong is the imperative in Matthew 28:19-20, and the collective instruction throughout the New Testament, that to ignore or neglect the Great Commission would be to undermine the wishes of Jesus. The commission was not only to the eleven apostles, but to all followers as well. While it was given in a specific time and place, the instructions were larger than that small band alone could accomplish in a lifetime. It must, therefore, be applied across the board to the followers of Jesus Christ throughout history.

F. F. Bruce writes of this passage, "Now His authority was world-wide and absolute, so their commission was given to the eleven as the representatives of the church to be. There are never good reasons for the Church's failing to reach out and go."[10]

The Great Commission of Christ held generational implications for the followers of Jesus. It is as important today as it was then. The mission is just as serious today as it was then. Each generation must rise to face the challenge, and go forth into the world to make disciples. Inherent in the instruction is the understanding that believers are to do as Christ did.

## Luke's Perspective

The example of the New Testament church stands as a paradigm for the local church. Churches are to do what Jesus did in His ministry. He came to, "seek and to save what was lost." There can be no room for error on this score. The local church and her members are to fulfill the Great Commission of Jesus Christ. As followers of Jesus Christ, a congregation is to be actively engaged in seeking the lost.

Luke 15 offers three parables, each with a main character who represents God. In each parable, something of value has been lost. The shepherd lost a sheep, the woman lost a coin, and the father lost a son. In the same way, those who are estranged from God matter to Him still. Lost people matter to God! They must, therefore, matter to the local church, and matter enough that all is done to find them.

At the Ascension, Jesus reiterated His command to the disciples. He told them what they would be, clearly. They were to be His witnesses. He told them as well, with what power they were moving into action: "But you will receive power when the Holy Spirit comes on you; and you will be my witnesses in Jerusalem, and in all Judea and Samaria, and to the ends of the earth" (Acts 1:8).

The locations Jesus gave (Jerusalem, Judea, Samaria, and the ends of the earth), can be symbolic of the methodology and approach each church could take. Starting within the own local environment, Christians are to move out "into an ever-extending series of concentric circles..."[11] Each region is to be evangelized with the gospel until the work has been completed. Still others suggest the passage implies that believers are to touch each of those areas concurrently with an evangelistic effort. Whether there is symbolism or a methodology behind the passage, the central message is clear and unmistakable—the Church, every believer and church, is to evangelize the world.

The immediate result of the coming of the Holy Spirit at Pentecost was the proclamation of the gospel and subsequent growth of the Church. From that point forward, there could be no confusion as to the purpose and intent of the apostles and the disciples. Those who would come to faith through their ministry would also take up the task and spread the gospel wherever they could. The people of the early church were united, filled with the Spirit, and mobilized for service; they took their stand for Christ, bore fruit, and proclaimed the good news. They were a people devoted to Christ. That devotion spurred them on to accomplish the mission given them. In the same way, modern churches must recapture that vision and respond accordingly.

At Pentecost, the believers, numbering only about 120 went out to communicate Christ.[12] Because of their empowerment and message, the Church grew rapidly as each one played a part. The disciples had gathered for prayer, been empowered, and went forth. When the persecution began following the stoning of Stephen, the Church was scattered but continued to preach and proclaim Christ.

More than just the apostles participated in the proclamation. The disciples, many of them new believers, took it upon themselves to witness to others. The local church needs to have such zeal and passion among today's believers. However, as Robert Logan and Thomas Clegg assert, "We tend to be more culturally sensitive in the 'Foreign mission field' but forget to be culturally sensitive 'at home' in the way we do church."[13]

The men, who had previously been ineffective, now were imbued with a passion for the purposes of Jesus Christ. They labored intensely, under adverse conditions, to fulfill their call. The evangelistic fervor was rooted and established in the local churches as they met and moved in their respective communities: "Those who accepted his message were baptized, and about three thousand were added to their number that day" (Acts 2:41).

The church kept track of those who were becoming followers of Jesus Christ. Those numbers were growing at an incredible rate, as they remained faithful to proclaim salvation through Jesus Christ.

Even in the face of persecution, the church continued to grow. Acts 2 provides an accounting of those who responded to Peter's sermon and were saved.

Another example of that is found in Acts 8:4, *"Those who had been scattered preached the word wherever they went."* Meaning, "proclaim, evangelize." The writings of Luke provide strong evidence for the fact that the Church was heavily involved in evangelism.

## John's Perspective

John records the appearance of Jesus following His resurrection. In that short time, of all the things Jesus could have said, He chooses to provide them with further instruction. John notes that Jesus again pointed His followers toward a specific task and mission. His disciples were being sent out to communicate the gospel. In John 20:21, Jesus says, *"Peace be with you! As the Father has sent me, I am sending you."*

The Father sent the Son into the world to redeem the world. His method would not change. Christ would in turn send His disciples into the world to spread the good news. That method should be no different today. God has used humankind and the church to proclaim the gospel down through the centuries. This modern era must reflect the willingness to be used in like manner.

## Paul's Perspective

Paul described in Romans 15:18-19 how he had been used to evangelize lost souls to lead *"the Gentiles to obey God by what I have said and done—by the power of signs and wonders, through the power of the Spirit of God.... I have fully proclaimed the good news of Christ."*

It was evident to Paul and to others that God had chosen him to take the gospel to the Gentiles. As he devoted his life toward that end, the fruit of his labors became significant. On more than one occasion, he risked life and limb to further the gospel. He encouraged others to follow his example and methods. His single-minded focus stands as a strong example and inspiration for the Church of today.

Paul wrote to the church at Corinth, *"...I have become all things to all people so that by all possible means I might save some"* (1 Corinthians 9:22). That passage reflects a "whatever it takes" attitude toward soul winning. Churches and church leadership would do well to emulate Paul's level of commitment to the cause. Paul approached the spreading of the gospel with the same zeal he had demonstrated toward Judaism.

Paul's life and actions were consumed by the strong desire and commitment to share Christ. He would take great risk, employ a variety of methods, and passionately proclaim Christ. His expectations and instructions were that others would follow suit. He instructed Timothy to engage in that great work. With the other responsibilities he had, evangelism was to remain a key focus: *"But you, keep your head in all situations, endure hardship, do the work of an evangelist, discharge all the duties of your ministry"* (2 Timothy 4:5).

The New Testament offers tremendous insight into the need for the local church to be evangelistically oriented. In addition to the biblical support, cross sections of past and present theologians weigh in on the subject as well. Their positions and statements help bring further clarity to the issue.

## Theological Perspectives

Millard Erickson writes that the call to evangelism is a command.[14] He further suggests that by submitting to Jesus Christ believers become obligated to do as he wishes. The biblical imperative having been sufficiently established leaves little room for those wishing to follow Christ. It was not an optional matter for them.[15] The disciples were commissioned as agents of Jesus Christ. As such, their mission was to follow His instructions and example.

Using Matthew 28:19 and Acts 1:8, Erickson states the mission was all-inclusive. All people groups were to be evangelized. He connects the faithfulness of the church to the Lord and the desire to bring Him joy, with the necessity of a strong evangelistic focus: "This involves going to people who we like and whom we may by nature tend to dislike. It extends to people who are unlike us, and it goes beyond our immediate sphere of contact and influence. In a real sense, local evangelism, church extension, or church planting and world missions are all the same thing."[16] The health and well-being of the church is dependent on its faithfulness to the evangelistic call.

The church was designed as an evangelistic instrument. Failing to function as designed will lead to a deterioration of its spiritual health. Perhaps the reason so many churches are stagnant or in decline relate to a lack of effective evangelistic efforts.

Lewis and Demarest, referenced previously, suggest in their *Integrative Theology,* the work of the church is to carry out God's purposes for the well-being of its members and the world. They write that the church should work for the reconciliation of everyone under the headship of Christ. The Church as a whole is the prime earthly agent of reconciliation with God's will.

Furthermore, Lewis and Demarest suggest that to reach the lost, the "found" in every generation ought to recruit, train, and deploy evangelists to make disciples in unreached areas of the world: "Every young person trained by the educational ministries of the church, and every adult church member, should know how to present the gospel of God's grace to people sensing their guilt and need."[17]

They further state that believers should be committed to the church that is devoted to God's purposes. They list four qualifications to seek in a church: "The church should be engaged in: communicating the Gospel by all ethical means to all person's in their locality, nation and world; promoting ministry involvement to edify others and evangelize the globe; manifesting both the gifts and the fruits of the Spirit in the church and the world; and cooperating with others who believe the same Gospel for the realization of Kingdom purposes."[18]

John Miley states in his Systematic *Theology* that the evangelism of the world is clearly the mission of Christianity. The fulfillment of that mission requires the Church because no one else can do it. He states further that it is a Christian duty that cannot be omitted. There would be no church but for that task. If ignored, the church would have no future nor could it have attained such a position in history.[19]

Miley questions what would have happened if the apostles decided not to evangelize or if others had enjoyed their private lives without consideration of the evangelistic task: "If men had neglected their duty toward this end in years past, then Christianity would have perished at its inception."[20] It seems possible that Miley's concern of 1892 is being lived out today by many churches. Sadly, acedia, or spiritual laziness, is not just a phenomenon among pastors. It can influence entire congregations who are lulled, lead, or enticed into less productive ministries or activities.

Paul Fetters writing in *Theological Perspectives* observes the need for the church to be actively engaged in evangelism. He states, "Under the superintendency of the Holy Spirit, the vital function of the church is evangelization."[21] The function of the church is restrictive. She is to be committed to proper work. Fetters points to the fact that disciples of Jesus Christ are more than just converts. They are individuals who obediently follow Jesus and carry out the great commission.

The Church is indeed to bear fruit in following the commands of Christ: "Anyone acknowledging the current cultural milieu, reading the myopic theologies of specific sociological issues, and listening to sermons on how to be healthy, wealthy and wise, can see the church runs the danger of unduly extending her task"; quoting Carl Barth, Fetters states the church should give focused attention to evangelism.[22]

Inherent in a focused effort is the idea of strategy. Jesus used strategies. He took teachable moments and maximized their use toward the end of changing hearts. The religious establishment had become ineffective and resulted in using law to control and keep those they already had. That is a terrible strategy, but one that repeatedly worms its way into the culture of churches.

Robert Coleman provides an excellent picture of the mission and goals that were so dear to Jesus Christ. Christ is the perfect example from which an understanding of evangelism may be drawn. Coleman notes that Jesus' objectives were clear. Jesus had planned to win and had ordered His life accordingly. He knew what His objectives were and labored to meet them.

Coleman says, as well, that as the Lord added daily to the church those who were being saved (Acts 2:47), the apostles were developing people to follow them: "The Acts of the Apostles is just the unfolding in the life of the growing church the principles of evangelism that have already been laid out in the life of Christ."[23]

The plan that Christ established was effective as evidenced by the success of the early church. There was a worldwide impact in a relatively short period. The cost was enormously high. Many people gave their lives for the gospel. The evangelistic furor was strong in those early years. Robert Coleman suggests that if the evangelistic fervor continued, the impact upon the world would have been even greater than it was. Nevertheless, as times moved on, there was a failure on the part of the church to continue that evangelistic mission with the passion and methods of Jesus Christ.

Robert Coleman provides John Wesley's theological perspective. He quotes Wesley, "It is not your business to preach so many times, and to take care of this or that society; but to save as many souls as you can; to bring as many sinners as you possibly can to repentance, and with all your power to build them up in that holiness without which they cannot see the Lord."[24]

William Barclay begins his book, *Fishers of Men,* with the following statement: "There can be nothing clearer and more unmistakable than the commission of the evangelist of Jesus Christ."[25] Additionally, he states the sphere in which the commission is to be carried out is nothing less than the whole world. Furthermore, the function of each Christian is to be part of the body of Christ, to be the agent, the hands, the feet, the mouth, the mind, and the heart through which Christ acts.[26]

## Consider...

*What point or points caught your attention as important and why?*

*What concept was new and requires additional time to process?*

*What action do you need to take as a result of what you read in this chapter?*

*What does the Holy Spirit say to you as you contemplate the chapter?*

*"The plan that Christ established was effective as evidenced by the success of the early church. There was a worldwide impact in a relatively short period."* In what ways have you witnessed local churches or the Church as a whole being unsuccessful in outreach efforts?

CHAPTER 3

# Step by Step

This book is not a "how to" manual. Rather, it provides a system that helps church and ministry leaders and others discover ways to reach specific groups with whom they have some affinity and may legitimately connect to move churches forward. It serves as an introduction to the STEP system. This book presents a seven STEP system for customizing an evangelistic framework. It serves as a guided, managed process. Through the system process, workable evangelistic initiatives are achieved. The system guides churches in determining which evangelistic methods or strategies would be most effective their specific context.

Before delving into each of the seven steps in the following chapters, the information in this chapter overviews very important aspects of the STEP system. You will be more than prepared to activate your church or ministry after reading and absorbing the wisdom shared throughout the remainder of the book.

The full implementation of the STEP system is a matter that requires diligent oversight. While it is conceptually simple, extreme complexities in the development of multilayered strategies and projects may be formed and executed successfully as a result of the study. Most churches will need significant guidance to complete the STEP system with full effectiveness. Comprehensive seminars on the methodology are available for those interested in significant kingdom-building effectiveness.

As you read further into the material, the STEP System is not for the faint of heart or the ill-prepared. Prior to moving forward, an extensive assessment of the leadership and support structures is necessary to determine if the congregation is ready for the STEP, and a healthy foundation exists. The pastor of the church or leader of the ministry is absolutely critical to the process, but nothing will be accomplished without the full engagement of the priesthood of believers.

The STEP system will not fit every congregation or ministry. While the overall aim is to provide an effective tool that any congregation can use, it will not address perhaps the most critical factor in the success of an evangelistic effort. The most critical factor has to do with the heart of the participants. A lack of passion for helping people connect to Jesus Christ limits the effectiveness of the project. Marginal results and mediocrity follow congregations not willing to put their collective energy into the effort. An organization with a weak foundation or splintered interests may suffer irreparable damage by moving forward without first ensuring sufficient foundational strength. There must be spiritual health and an overt sense of passion and desire to advance the Kingdom of God.

A lack of passion for the things of God, the mission of God, the desires of God, reflect a fundamental error birthed in the heart and the mind. It reflects a lack of understanding about the grace through which salvation comes and the abundant love we receive from Christ. It reflects an imbalance in concerns, priority, drive, and significance of life in general. It reflects our darker nature, consumed more by our own wants and needs than the wants and desires emanating from the throne room of God, and spilling over into the sacred Book that serves as our guide.

At the core, a lack of passion significant enough to motivate every believer to a deep desire to serve begins in the heart. It's a problem Scripture talks about as well: *"These people honor me with their lips but their hearts are far from me"* (Matthew 15:8). Those who align with the purposes of God, surrender their agendas and desires to the extent that is consistent with the will of God.

## Spiritual Warfare

Spiritual warfare is real and will manifest during the process of developing evangelistic strategies. It highlights the importance of a single soul, and the battle that is necessary to bring them out of darkness and into the light. The enemy will fight to keep them in the dark. To march into the battle zone with a naïve view of the enemy's efforts, is to invite disaster. Conversions are part of the Church's work in the world. The Church must face attacks head-on, and see them for what they are—battles for the souls of men, women, and children. Evil is never to be appeased. It is to be confronted, dealt with, and overcome.

A basic understanding about the legitimacy of spiritual warfare is necessary. Significant work on that subject exists, and is a precursor to strategy development. An in-depth examination of spiritual warfare and perhaps a solid Bible study on the subject is suggested. The most prepared fellowships will have equipping on the subject of intense prayer and spiritual warfare. Please, do not take this suggestion lightly.

Teams that do not have the desire to become a transformational agent of redemption, should not engage in the process. A catalytic leader is necessary to spark commitment and action from the congregants. The leaders build up the priesthood of believers and encourage. They train and prepare. They care for their congregant's injuries in battle. They forgive their shortcomings and failures and move them closer and closer to missional objectives.

Ask yourself, *Is missional success occurring now in our local church context? If not, why not?* If a change is needed, bring it. If greater skill and competencies are required, go get them. Accept nothing less than the singular focus of Kingdom expansion through the priesthood of believers.

The enemy is real and has dropped bits of poison all over culture. The Church is not immune to his influence. The lack of cultural influence is reflective, in part, on the infiltration of ideas and interests that keep our collective focus on things other than the core of our mission. The level of spiritual warfare is massive. The extent to which we casually disregard the implication reflects our lack of catalytic engagement. Social ills are the playground of the enemy.

The following are a few cases that dominate our culture now and represent a clear attack on biblical Christianity.

"In 2014, one of the top priorities of the homosexual agenda was, and remains, to prohibit and outlaw *conversion therapy,* particularly for teenagers. California and New Jersey are the only states to have enacted such laws (Governor Chris Christie signed it into law as he was preparing his reelection campaign), and leftists are pushing similar bans in many other states now.

In a speech on December 10, 2013, to a pro-family rally in Jamaica, Brian Camenker, of the organization Mass Resistance, outlined the step-by-step approach of the homosexual agenda:

1. Legalize homosexuality
2. Promote gay pride parades
3. Demand non-discrimination laws
4. Insist on homosexuals' adoption of children
5. Push the homosexual agenda in schools
6. Force "gay marriage" on society
7. Demand public funding to deal with increased homosexual-related social problems
8. Promote the transgender agenda
9. Impose a large-scale loss of free speech
10. Ban counseling for kids confused by homosexual issues
11. Attack churches[1]

*The Washington Post* has been attacking Christians for their stance on traditional, biblical views on marriage. Thomas D. Williams, PhD, wrote the following in a July 12, 2016 article titled, "Washpo Attacks Christian Leaders as 'Enemies of Equality'" "In a macabre hit piece, the *Washington Post* has launched a smear campaign against important Christian leaders who espouse Biblical morality on homosexuality, labeling them as 'enemies of equality.'"[2]

The nature of the warfare is not always obvious nor acknowledged by the systems and mechanisms within churches. Sometimes we clean up or sanitize a battleground, and redefine it as something manageable by and belonging to "the professionals." Hence, we do not have to deal with it as a function of the body as a whole. Our denominational silos prevent the very unity in the body that serves as a catalyst for biblical principles shaping culture. Some believers have gone so far as to adopt a holy disengagement from culture. While we are in the world but not of it, we are none-the-less "in the world." We are here for a purpose. The calling of the catalytic leader is to do something more. This leader steps into the cultural arena with the only answer for humanity—leadership is critical. We need bold leadership that intelligently engages the STEP system and provides an advantage in planning and developing evangelistic ministries.

## Team Selection

The team selection process begins with an application of interest. Assessments follow the completion of an application. A determination is made concerning readiness of the local church to engage in such a ministry. The implications are potentially deep for the congregation that decides to get into the arena and commit to the process. Prior to moving forward organizationally, participating teams will need additional preparation and coaching, available through an intensive training process that incorporates team development and class time. Team building occurs in a variety of formats, customizable to the needs of the organization. To insure the highest degree of preparation, we recommend pastors and ministry leaders participate in the teambuilding experience together.

## Implementation

The design of the STEP system requires implementation over a minimum twelve-week period. There are seven STEPs, with work accomplished prior to and following each step. That does not mean that some of the strategies developed only last twelve weeks. Rather, that is the minimum time allocated to the process and formation of strategies for deployment. Once teams are assembled, strategies implementation begins. Subsequent evaluations occur as quickly as possible. The nature of the strategy requires taking a short view in methodology, and a longer view in some instances. The results, do not always come about quickly. Positive results with a flood of people coming to Christ do not always come about quickly.

In some cases, a significant amount of time and several sequential efforts are needed to achieve conversions. However, it is possible to have immediate results. It depends on which evangelistic strategies are employed. A debriefing of participants helps in assessing strengths and weaknesses of the STEP system, and provides guidance for making any necessary changes. The mindset of any system is to commit to making continual improvements and adaptations as the environment changes and social transitions warrant.

## Long-Term, Short-Term Evangelism

It is important to observe that many of our evangelism efforts in churches today seem to be short-term initiatives. Our ability to affect cultural change and promulgate Christian values, attitudes, beliefs, and expectations is diminished by a focus only on short-term efforts. It is critical that we realize there are both short and long-term strategies that should be brought to bear on church culture in order to effectuate a more permanent and impactful shift. The enemies of Christian faith, biblical principles, and the wonderful message of redemption use the long game to gain incremental usurpation of culture. The forces of evil do not play fair.

## Generational Concerns

The lives of future generations—their souls and spiritual well-being—are harmed by the degree to which we fail to develop a strong cultural and spiritual foundation, receptive to the ideas and notions consistent with Christian belief and practice. We diminish significant opportunity and future effectiveness. It is our responsibility to properly steward the very culture entrusted to us. It is our work to till the soil, remove the weeds, eliminate the rocks, and properly amend the soil for the seed to effectively grow when planted. It is our role to keep the vultures from snatching the seeds from the mouths of babes. It is our responsibility to protect against the encroachment of an enemy that labors to destroy.

As shepherds, it is our responsibility to not only care for the sheep currently in our fold, but to care for the cultural environment in which future generations will be added to the fold. When we allow the filth of opposing ideologies, principles, values of secular humanism, atheism, and social degradation to go unchallenged, we merely are allowing the weeds to grow, the rocks to accumulate, and feed for the cultural vultures of the day to pluck away any seed sown. Think of our negligence as aid and comfort to the enemy as he steals life from the most innocent, the children of future generations. When we fail to build and maintain a healthy culture receptive to Christian teaching and principles, we jeopardize future generations. This is unacceptable. We are the guardians, we are the Church, the Body of Christ.

*We are therefore Christ's ambassadors, as though God were making his appeal through us... (2 Corinthians 5:20).*

In order to secure the long-term environment receptive to a Christian message, we have to be willing to fight on every front. We have everything at our disposal to demolish every argument that sets itself up against godliness. What seems to have occurred in recent years is reflective of collective cowardice displayed against those enemies of virtue that have roared and shouted loudly against Christian views and culture. We have allowed, for example, our tax-exempt status to silence our views from the pulpit to the pew. We drank the "proverbial Kool Aid," and allowed ourselves to be effectively silenced. This also is unacceptable.

*For though we live in the world, we do not wage war as the world does. The weapons we fight with are not the weapons of the world. On the contrary, they have divine power to demolish strongholds. We demolish arguments and every pretension that sets itself up against the knowledge of God, and we take captive every thought to make it obedient to Christ (2 Corinthians 10:3-5).*

There must be a corresponding willingness to engage society to counter ideologies that threaten the welfare of future generations, and our ability to communicate successfully in culture. Our enemy, on the other hand, is extremely aggressive in undermining the secure foundations of the principles, attitudes, beliefs, and expectations that are part of the Judeo/Christian worldview.

Until recently in this country's history, Christian views had been inculcated into the cultural fabric. The strategy of anti-Christian bigotry has been to undermine virtually any concept of the sacred in exchange for purely secular notions within the society. The success that side has achieved is a testimony to our failure to hold the line, aggressively build our forces, and strategically advance the gospel. We have made the work in which we have been called far more difficult simply by ignoring the incremental strategies and attacks brought to bear on Christian belief in the public arena. Our culture today is a far cry from what was anticipated and desired by those who fled the constrictive societies and governments of Europe in pursuit of religious freedom.

## Most Effective Form of Evangelism

It is widely held that the most effective form of evangelism is personal evangelism that occurs between people on a one-to-one basis. Most of us believe that having a personal relationship with an individual can open doors of opportunity wherein we can express our views of Jesus Christ and the saving knowledge that is available to all who would believe.

A key principle of the STEP system, is to find doors through which people willingly enter, and from which relationships can be established and the gospel shared. Rather than the Church knocking on the door of an individual to evangelize them, we must find doors that the unchurched and de-churched person wants to enter.

Scores of books emphasizing the role of "friendship evangelism" have been published, curriculum developed, and put into practice. The objective after someone comes to saving knowledge of Jesus Christ, is then to grow in that relationship. We are to make disciples, which entails in part, an educational function. Growth occurs through study. A component of the growth of believers is the extent to which they are engaged in the Word.

Short-term evangelism must include a certain intentionality in building up the disciples in the faith. Otherwise, they will tend to fall away or adopt other patterns of belief and practice, which in the end undermines the strength of their Christian life. An additional aim of the disciple-making process is growing the believer to maturity. There are several areas needed in the life of the disciple to which we need to give attention: spiritual growth, intellectual growth, commitment level, and faith maturity are all essential components in preparing disciples.

Standard methodologies and practices within many churches include life groups, simple invitations, friendship development, and family opportunities. Youth programs can be effective instruments through which parents are attracted to a local church and become part of a congregation. Those methodologies are already widely practiced; yet long-term results are mixed. Toward that end, we must develop an understanding of and a drive for cultural fluency, so the Body of Christ will become culturally savvy. The long-term approach requires it.

It seems as if the Church reacts to and follows cultural trends, rather than proactively positioning for leadership in culture. That must shift. It is very difficult to have influence from a distance.

Rather than react to culture, which dominates much of the activities within the church today, we need to be culturally proactive. In order to be proactive, we must aggressively take steps that build a great awareness of the societies in which we live. We can no longer afford to fear those points of culture at which we are dissimilar and do not reflect Christian values. Rather, we must become students of, engaged with, and influential in those aspects of culture that we have previously kept at arm's length. We cannot acquiesce to fear. We cannot allow our disapproval of certain aspects of culture to keep us from having influence in those cultures. It is time to engage and get into the arena. This is a dangerous proposition. Some people are too susceptible to the influences and temptations of the dark side of culture.

We have to be careful in selecting who will do what in those aspects of culture that we have traditionally not engaged. What is strikingly different from times in the recent past, is if we did engage at some level in a ministry opportunity, we did so on our terms. Gaining an awareness of culture and gaining cultural fluency and literacy requires us to enter not on our terms, but on the terms of those involved and engaged in the subculture. That was the tactic of Christ.

## An Instrument of Communicatio

The church is an instrument of communication. Redemption occurs when we communicate effectively. The church has traditionally communicated in a particular context. The context is within a particular culture. The culture is the place in which the message either resonates or fails to connect. Culture is behavior, values, attitudes, beliefs, and expectations by which a group shares and lives. Those values, attitudes, beliefs, and expectations shape the understanding of the collective. They are held in common and perpetuated by the collective. Culture can be entrenched firmly within a people group, or pliable in the face of significant effective pre-suppositional challenges. Social structures, practices, and decision making are informed by the greater cultural components. Culture functions as a guide to life decisions, purchases, governance, and industry. It is the collective will in both function and dysfunction.

Cultural fluency is an ability, coupled with a determination, which when paired with spiritual giftedness, aids in understanding as much about a particular culture as possible. The leader is a student, interpreter of, and an expert in cultural trends at each level of the social fabric. That knowledge translates into strategic approaches to advance the Kingdom.

The prophetic voice is tied to understanding culture. The gospel message is relevant to and transformational in communication of truth born out of the depths of spiritual connectedness and informed by cultural understanding, then wisely applied. It is made applicable in transformative ways through spiritual wisdom ultimately tied to the presence of the Holy Spirit present within.

Culture varies from nation to nation, state to state, and within the wide array of subcultures. Subcultures themselves have a context, language, actions, and activities that are best interpreted and understood by those within them. There are instances when emersion within the culture and subcultures are the only means by which someone gains understanding with strategic and transformative power. This is the point that the Church today continues to lose significant ground and demonstrates little tolerance for correction. The trajectory of the Church in the USA within the past fifty years has led to more and more social isolation and ineffective strategies to mitigate those losses.

As we have witnessed within the past thirty years, the impact of technological advancement holds extraordinarily substantial power to transform culture. The catalytic leader is determined to understand those culturally relevant issues, within which the mission is to be advanced.

Our objective is to create a desire among leaders to become culture watchers as an instrument by which the Kingdom is advanced. The desire to rise to such a level of proficiency must first be born in the seat of the heart. The compelling rationale for such a desire must be strong enough to drive leaders to proficiency and expertise, which will find its way into communicating redemptive truth. That truth is derived from a strong desire and brought to bear through scriptural application of truth to culture.

John Clawson states that a leader, "Seeing what needs to be done, understanding ALL the underlying forces at play, has the courage to initiate action to make things better."[3]

The scope of our leadership knowledge base within nationwide churches is not as extensive as it could be. I acknowledge that this book is not a final answer to the question of competency, but rather a humble addition to the already extensive and brilliant insights within the field of evangelism. Recognizing the times in which we now live, and the challenges we face as the Church in America specifically, this book is predicated on certain observations and trends, which need addressed, and the development of leaders is part of the process.

## Lagging Behind

The majority of churches tend to lag behind societal trends. It is a primary failure of the church today and is symptomatic of our lack of interest in cultural understanding. It further magnifies the gap in our social influence. The church does not set the social trends. As it is, ideologies with less to offer humanity, have infiltrated the epicenters of cultural influence. The resultant social shift has displaced Christian ideals. Culture has so radically changed, and our systems so lagged behind, that our message gives the appearance of being irrelevant and of little consequence. Almost to the extent that Christians and our faith in practice is a parody of ourselves. Public perception is such.

Rather than acquiesce to such notions, our focus, energy, and effort should be redirected to actions that provide the potential for greatest impact in the shortest period of time, with the likelihood of longer term success and sustained advancement.

"Leaders must continually work to broaden their vision and deepen their insight into global, societal, market, competitive, and consumer related issues that surround any organization," says James Clawson[4]

The church of tomorrow will stretch the limits of cultural understanding, so as to effectuate influence. There is neither the time for nor the place for laziness in the matter. Understanding *all* the underlying forces at play, is not an easy undertaking. For example, the average pastor, trained in even the best seminary, will often have only those skills relevant to understanding the Scripture, the life of the church, and a cursory review of contextualized leadership training. The point here is not to minimalize the importance of theological training. To the contrary, the point is that training needs to go much further if we sincerely wish to develop the skills and competencies needed for church and ministry leaders to lead beyond the scope of their own organizational systems.

Not too unlike those who study for an MBA, trained clergy will face a myriad of challenges where the education received is only partially applicable to situations and issues that arise. On the job training occurs for even the best prepared. Additionally, knowing what constitutes *all* of the underlying forces at play requires us to breach ideologically, philosophically, and practically the competencies engrained into the ethos of theological education and the systems and churches who support them.

A pastor or ministry leader can be measured a success by internal measures of compliance to traditions that may, ironically, reinforce the overall downward trends in the cultural influence. While the pastoral leader finds some measure of approval within the church, church attendance as a whole in the USA is in decline, due in part to a larger, cultural measure that has radically shifted, and which leaders are unaware of or ill-prepared to address, given the pressure to comply with outdated metrics.

Similarly, a Christian businessperson can be measured a success by the standards of the industry in which engaged. However, the effective integration of faith and witness within the vocation may be an area of struggle. Often, and appropriately so, it seems there is a certain degree of expectation that the church will provide people with the tools for effective integration of faith into the public arena. That the church itself is ill-prepared to effectively equip for strategic integration of the faith into the public arena, the cycle continues and the trends downward gain momentum.

Of course, there are exceptions to these phenomena. There are churches within the country that influence culture through the work of the church and the strategic integration of Kingdom principles in the lives of its people. But the trend we are now experiencing as a whole, is far from reversing.

## Advancing Kingdom Work

Advancing Kingdom work is the core function of the believer and the measure of measures. The means by which that is achieved varies in part by vocation. The church needs a comprehensive, catalytic shift by which it and those who are part of the church gain an appropriate level of commitment to their call as believers. That shift begins with the leader.

As a church or ministry leader unfolds the Scriptures to their adherents, the relevance to current cultural issues may be difficult if not ardent students of culture, at all its unsavory levels, with an eye capable of seeing and understanding culture at each level and in all places. Each follower of Christ should know the context of their own culture. But too often it seems there is a desire to pretend we are islands, and we tend to our own beach, and pretend the rest of culture, especially the darker side of culture, either does not exist, or remains hidden from view.

In reality, we are on the same beach. As long as we pretend that what happens in the underbelly of culture has no impact on culture, we will continue to lose ground in culture. By not strategically communicating the good news in every corner of society—the only truly transformational message known—we will continue to get the same results.

W. Edward Deming had this to say about successful leadership:

> Every organization is perfectly designed to produce the results it is producing. Many if not most people do not learn from their happenings/experiences, they simply repeat what they have always done. Many people are not mindful of their surroundings or their experiences. They go through life in a kind of a fog. In other words, they become too routinized to see opportunity and challenge.[5]

Understanding *all* the underlying forces at play requires a catalytic leader in pastoral ministry to broaden their knowledge base in a multiple of disciplines. A Christian businessperson, physician, attorney, engineer, etc., desiring to be a leader in the mission of the Church also faces a significant challenge. His or her effectiveness may correlate with their knowledge of spiritual matters.

Part of the reason for decline in cultural impact in North America is due to a casual spirituality that expects little of its adherents and perpetuates systems that fail to deploy followers to passionate spirituality in the marketplace. The Christian leader of tomorrow will need a sound understanding of the issues beyond those of the seminary. The Christian leader in other disciplines will possess a sound understanding of spiritual, biblical principles, and cultural issues, well beyond the scope of their own discipline.

## Christian Leaders...

The following list is not exhaustive, but merely a brief but significant body of knowledge required for catalytic levels of effectiveness.

- Christian leaders need a more-than-casual grasp of the social fabric in which they live. A Christian leader will have an understanding of the social structure, support systems, agencies, methods and practices, as well as an understanding about how the community deals comprehensively with the social ills and strengths.

Society, whether we like it or not, is an integration of a wide variety of interests, activities, and life philosophies. Some of those interests and activities are in direct conflict with one another, and some function only on the periphery and outside the general knowledge of the populace. There is a collective will operant in every society. That will, or personality, is reflected in the culture and belies the extent to which a comprehensive, cohesive understanding exists and the degree to which solutions are brought to bear upon the whole.

- Christian leaders will make themselves aware of the culture at all levels, and as deeply as possible. We must bring to bear the collective insights from cultural practitioners. The Christian leader, steps into the arena, and goes where others will not. They are ready for the fight, but fighting with spiritual tools—yet at strategic times, using the tools of the world.

- Christian leaders realize that while we fight against principalities and powers, the battle is often played out and manifested in society, right before our eyes. Too often we have grown calloused and removed from the brutality of the battle. Below the surface of our isolated sanctuaries, lives are in ruin through the instrumentality of evil forces at play. In cities and towns in the Midwest, human trafficking wages war against human dignity. On East Coast highways, drugs move from state to state, north to south. Gross abuse of children occurs in communities all across the nation. Christian leaders cannot allow atrocities go unchallenged.

- Christian leaders engage. There are IEDs, so to speak, planted everywhere to trap and snare the naïve. The Christian leader is anything but naïve. The level of spiritual warfare is massive. The extent to which we casually disregard the implication reflects our lack of Christian engagement. Social ills are the playground of the enemy.

- Christian leaders must be willing to understand culture before we can confront. Knowledge of culture will determine how we confront. Culture is our context. It is the battlefield in which we engage. The enemy is at work in regions and places we fear to look or travel. Christian leaders will gain intelligence on enemy strongholds. They will not fear the enemy or the person who operates for them, regardless of position or lack thereof.

- Christian leaders will not pretend evil does not exist, or believe that they cannot exert influence of redemption within even the darkest realm of human and spiritual depravity. Rather, we will risk it all for the only cause with any eternal permanence. Even if it means challenging the ineffective systems of denominational protocols. Christian leaders are emissaries of God—agents of redemption. Human constructs hold sway only to that point where alignment with God is hindered.

  The world is open to astute leaders who desire to understand all the levels of their immediate culture. From the social fabric of industry, money and banking, legal and social services, to the darker side of society of vices, drugs, sexual behavior, and even criminal sexual deviances. The ability to grasp the culture, possess an understanding, and resolve to fight its ills are at their fingertips. At no other time in history has an opportunity to delve deeply into the support structure as well as the underbelly of social degradation, been so readily available. Information is everywhere. Every organization advertises their societal function.

- The Internet exists, at present, as a key to the world of social structures and subcultures. While Christian leaders are not interested in prurient satisfaction, they are interested in bringing redemption to every facet of society. They are fixated on a greater purpose. The information gained is to move the Christian leader into an informed position of strength for the intention of executing redemptive initiatives and strategies.

- Christian leaders have a high calling. That calling is not only for those in the pastoral role. We are a royal priesthood. We are all called into the arena. The arena is the battleground. It is the place where war is waged in a confined space. It is the place where every ounce of ability is challenged and tested. It is the place where we are brought face to face with our weaknesses and strengths. It is the place where every tool of the enemy is brought to bear upon our mission. It is the place where the enemy will stop at nothing to stop our progress. It is the place where the victor gains an advantage by digging deeply within. It is the place where God sustains us beyond our capability. It is the place where He brings the only answer and solution for humanity.

- Christian leaders of tomorrow will understand the past, the trends of today, and the underlying assumptions of those within the political seats of power. The data and evidence regarding the direction and values of culture and the various concepts and theories that are perpetuated ideologically within the seats of power in a culture are all available to the discerning eye. Christian leaders should be able to discern inferences and interpret the signs of the cultural trends. The church of tomorrow will understand the pressing social mores, the redefinition of acceptable behaviors, and the laws that are brought to bear to enforce the acceptance of those behaviors, particularly the behaviors in conflict with scriptural understanding.
- Christian leaders will also be students of the power structures. That level of understanding will help the church to engage in aggressive positioning at the epicenters of social control. We must assert ourselves in the area of academics, law, media, medicine, ethics, and social institutions. Our strategy needs to be comprehensive for societal engagement and a combination of both overt and covert operations.

Such a long-term view of evangelism and the requirements to become effective in that field is the missing component in the scope of the activities in which a church engages. We must become students of culture, engage culture, seed every level with Christian values, collaborate and unite with others who share core values, and bring influence through the active engagement of every Christian in every field of endeavor. Aligning with organizations that reflect our values, helps pull the community of faith together and thus spread a redemptive message and saturate culture.

This book is designed to move us in that direction and create an opportunity for both short-term and long-term repositioning. We are undertaking a mission that when effectively employed and deployed will help the local church form strategic, targeted, and evangelistic plans.

## Consider...

*What point or points stuck out to you as important and why?*

*What concept was new and requires additional time to process?*

*In your opinion, what action needs taken as a result of what you read?*

*What does the Holy Spirit say to you as you contemplate the chapter?*

*"Rather, we must become students of, engaged with, and influential in those aspects of culture that we have previously kept at arm's length. We cannot acquiesce to fear. We cannot allow our disapproval of certain aspects of culture to keep us from having influence in those cultures." How willing are you to engage in this arena?*

CHAPTER 4

# Step One: Strategic Foundation

## Holy-Spirit, Rock-Solid Firm

The STEP system, while structured, is only to be used in conjunction with the guidance of the Holy Spirit. Prayer is the truest foundation through which God directs and moves. Each phase of the process is subordinate to the will of God as He reveals His desires through the prayerful body. It is easy to get caught up in the systems and planning. We must embrace caution to ensure we are in alignment with God's desire as we move forward. However, overanalyzing slows the process. There is no strategy that is superior to the enabling of direct, Holy Spirit influence.

Prayer requesting the guidance and active presence of the Holy Spirit is the most solid building block of an evangelistic effort. Believing in the guidance of the Holy Spirit with a willingness to go wherever He so directs; that reality includes listening to when the audience should be and when God wants to be involved.

> *Therefore put on the full armor of God, so that when the day of evil comes, you may be able to* **stand your ground,** *and after you have done everything, to* **stand. Stand firm** *then, with the belt of truth buckled around your waist, with the breastplate of righteousness in place, and with your feet fitted with the readiness that comes from the gospel of peace (Ephesians 6:13-15).*

## Overview

A firm foundation for successfully reaching the goal of advancing the Kingdom through the STEP system is built on assessing potential team participants. Unlike many evangelistic efforts, the foundation phase begins with an assessment of the people engaged, on a number of different levels. It is an extensive data-gathering exercise requiring tabulation. For some, the assessment determines who can work most effectively together, and what types of people should not be teammates. The purpose is to reduce opportunity for negative personality conflicts and increase the likelihood of effective team building. Assessments also determine the strengths and giftedness of team members and includes evangelistic preferences and temperament, conflict resolution, and a myriad of developmental considerations.

What follows is additional foundational information to consider, providing supplementary insight for the leader.

## Pre-determine Individual Interests

## Data

To be effective, an evangelistic effort needs data. In a sense, the entire process is reliant on continual data being provided at each step so that critical decision making can be effective.

Data Point 1: One of the fastest ways to gather information is to survey the group of believers—congregation, ministry group, etc. The initial survey is a very simple exercise in finding various points of personal interests. The leader needs to know the specific interests of those involved. Every individual has something they are passionate about. All that is required is directing those passions in an evangelistic direction. Part of the strategy is to tap into those areas that will heighten "buy in" to the effort by leveraging the passion for an activity they already possess. Many people cannot see the ways in which their activities can easily convert to an effective point of strategic outreach. There is often a disconnect between someone's personal points of interest and the notion of using that interest for Kingdom purposes.

## Social Media

Social media sites can be used for data mining. Facebook, for example, tends to foster a high degree of interpersonal connectivity. Personal profiles often show the various interests of those who use it. Those interests are potential connecting points with others who share similar interests. LinkedIn and other social media channels may also reveal useful data. The "blog world" opens a myriad of connecting points on multiple subjects and interests. Categorizing those interests into subculture data points can help uncover trends. Strong trends of similar interests can provide opportunities with higher levels of immediate impact and increased engagement.

The survey questions are provided later, as the leader needs to till the soil prior to administering the survey. There will be resistance. There will be some within the congregation or group who will respond immediately. There will be others who resist the attempt at soliciting their participation. There will be outright opposition. Christian leaders must move forward with the forces they have, with the level of "buy in" from the committed who desire to be part of the work of God and move in alignment.

There are seven levels of potential involvement. The levels are placed in order from lower to highest:

7. Active resistance
6. Passive resistance
5. Apathy
4. Compliance
3. Agreement
2. Engagement
1. Passion

Unfortunately, those in the lowest form of participation will resist through open assault. Both the leader and participants should expect resistance to surface and be prepared to face it. Some resistance is sinfulness. Some will be a manifestation of the enemy trying to thwart an initiative.

The team, and specifically the leader, should be aware of the tactics that could be deployed against an evangelical effort and prayerfully engage accordingly. *Passive resistance* will manifest by quiet lack of engagement, acknowledgment or participation. *Apathy* is much the same, and *Compliance* is out of duty. *Agreement* is at least some sense of willingness, and *Engagement* is born out of heart and desire. Passion is a recognition of calling, in which all else is secondary.

The leader will want teams established on which level 1 and 2 members participate. The leader will look for participants who live "inside out," meaning the highest concern is for alignment with God's purposes. People who live "outside in" are too driven by issues of ego and fear of rejection. They may also be driven by surface-level desires, which will not be sufficient to sustain them through difficult trials.

Inside-out motivators are deep, heart-felt drivers that come from a love of God and a desire to see Him work.

John Kotter provides critical insight to leading an effort. He defines leadership as the process of moving a group or groups in some direction through mostly noncoercive means. Effective leadership produces movement in the long term best interest of the group.[1] He provides a four-point solution to guide the process:

1. Develop a bold new vision.
2. An intelligent, that is, workable strategy for implementing the vision.
3. Eliciting the cooperation and teamwork from a large network of essential people.
4. Relentless work to keep key people in the network motivated toward the vision.

Great vision emerges when a powerful mind, working long and hard on massive amounts of information, is able to see interesting patterns and new possibilities.[2]

The team tallies the data-gathered results and identifies the most likely potential connecting points and audiences. As part of the process, it is important to understand that prayer undergirds each aspect. Discernment also plays a significant role. The smaller group of STEP participants work through an exercise assigning point values to potential evangelistic efforts provided by the congregation or group.

The team then chooses among the highest three options. Limiting the effort to three is the most difficult aspect of any initiative. But trying to do too much with too few resources results in aggravation, frustration, and burnout. Achieving some small victories serves to encourage participants down the road. Starting small and growing seems more realistic than attempting too many efforts at once. Subsequent steps will be in vain if there is not a collective will and the necessary skill to execute the plan. Many plans fail in the execution phase.

Larry Bossidy and Ram Charan offer insights to mitigate the opportunity for failure. According to them, any group moving an initiative forward needs to consider philosophical keys to effective execution:

1. Execution is a discipline and integral to any strategy.
2. Execution is the major role of the leader.
3. Execution must be the core element of the organizational.
4. Reward the doers.
5. Expand people's capabilities.
6. Know yourself culture.[3]

They go on to say there are three building blocks of successful execution.[4] Building Block One requires the leader to exhibit seven essential characteristics:

1. Know your people and business
2. Insist on realism
3. Set clear goals and priorities
4. Follow through
5. Reward the doers
6. Expand capabilities
7. Know yourself

Building Block Two is creating a framework for cultural change. The STEP system represents a fundamental shift in how to accomplish evangelism within the context of a local church or ministry. It offers a framework that challenges at another level. That level is the mind. The need to eliminate the self-defeating behaviors and myopic organizational determinism that locks churches into status quo level thinking must be broken within the internal culture. Emphasizing possibilities over practicality can move the culture forward. The level of thinking necessary to move the interior culture to external cultural influence is worth examining.

| EXECUTING TIPS | AUDIENCE | OPTION 1 | OPTION 2 |
|---|---|---|---|
| TEAM | | | |
| TACTIC | | | |
| TIMELINE | | | |
| INTELLIGENCE | | | |
| INSIGHTS | | | |
| INVESTMENT | | | |
| PRAYER | | | |
| PROCESS | | | |
| PRODUCTIVITY | | | |

This TIPS grid helps to clarify specific actions relative to specific audiences. The team is the collection of people brought to one audience in some aspect of the strategy. The right team members in the right role for the right reasons sets the tone for the balance of redemptive focus. The tactics will vary from audience to audience and should be designed with the specific audience in mind. Timelines can be confusing. It is bad judgment to force a timeline that will require action without the foundational level of fact finding and strategy development.

The gathering of information, along with insightful use of that information, can mean the success of the venture. Prayer undergirds everything. A sensitivity to the Holy Spirit is the most critical aspect of the entire strategy. We cannot presume upon the Holy Spirit to bless our endeavors if we have failed to seek His will and guidance. The process is determined by the specific nature of the audience, and which actions may bring about the greatest opportunity for success.

Productivity is the bottom line result. Too many ministry efforts attract some level of participation of those outside the church, but many activities of the church do not result in the primary function of the church being achieved—souls coming to faith in Jesus Christ. We have to be honest with ourselves, and critical of our failures. The bottom line question we all must answer—are the greatest number of people being saved through our ministry initiatives?

Ray Kroc, of McDonalds fame, pushed the envelope of what others thought could be achieved. Kroc was the visionary. His financial manager was Harry Sonneborn. They were opposite ends of the spectrum. One was practical, the other visionary. In Kroc's world, the practical served the vision, not the other way around. There is an expected gap between what is "reasonable" to the visionary, and what is "reasonable" to the practical-driven, numbers cruncher. There is very little room for fear in mission execution. Kroc lived his values and focused on what could be achieved, not what could *not* be achieved. He valued vision. Conviction, flexibility, cooperation, enthusiasm, toleration of dissent, mentoring, optimism, and giving—all those values, active within a congregation or group leveraged upon a mission, can bring the impossible into the realm of the possible.

Building Block Three is consistent with the notions of Jim Collins in his book, *Good to Great*. The right people must be in the right place. Or in Collin's language, have the right people in the bus in the right seat.[5]

## Prayer Support

The prayerful identification of a potential audience begins before the first step, in the context of worship, newsletters, and other printed announcements. The congregation enlist participants for prayer support efforts to undergird the process and provide data the group would consider in making strategic decisions.

The underlying assumption is that many churches experience only marginal evangelistic results because they had not clearly defined their goal or target audience, and thus failed to deliver an effective effort. In the event that they may target a specific audience to reach, the strategies employed often do not fit the target. The entire process needs the support of prayer as the participants seek guidance in determining appropriate targets.

The New Testament themes are clear: evangelism is the central task of the Body of Christ. Lost people matter to God. He labored for them, and the Church exists to fulfill that mission in every period of time. Each generation must rise to meet the challenge.

With the examination of biblical passages, certain principles and characteristics develop that add further understanding and application to the local church and her mission. Christ's example in both word and deed clearly demonstrates His commitment to reach lost souls. His ministry was a ministry of reconciliation and redemption. Those who identify themselves with His name must also embrace His purpose. Lost people matter to God and must matter to the local church. If His example were not enough, His commands provide instruction.

Those who desire to live an authentic Christian life that reflects the values of Christ will want to be obedient to His commands. Deep, heartfelt gratitude for salvation finds expression through obedience to the commandments and teachings of Christ. It is the measure that Christ Himself points to: *"If you love me, keep my commands"* (John 14:15). Some choose what commands they will in fact obey, but if both His words and deeds pointed to an area of passion, clearly we could conclude the church is to do likewise.

If the church is to live out the passage in Galatians, believer's lives will reflect the very same values as Christ: "I have been crucified with Christ and I no longer live, but Christ lives in me. The life I live in the body, I live by faith in the Son of God, who loved me and gave himself for me" (Galatians 2:20).

The guiding paradigm is Christ, the apostles, the New Testament church, and their evangelistic zeal. It is obvious what value Jesus placed on reconciling people to the Father. From the incarnation of Christ, to the cross and resurrection, a purpose was at work.

That purpose was to restore fellowship between humankind and God through Jesus Christ. The attitude of believers toward the will of God must reflect that of Christ Himself:

> *In your relationships with one another, have the same mindset as Christ Jesus: Who, being in very nature God, did not consider equality with God something to be used to his own advantage; rather he made himself nothing by taking the very nature of a servant, being made in human likeness. And being found in appearance as a man, he humbled himself by becoming obedient to death—even death on a cross! (Philippians 2:5-8).*

Considering the example, the commands, and the expectations of Christ for His followers, believers must respond with their lives and commit to evangelistic efforts within the local churches. Such a focus reflects the heart of Christ. The full impact of the New Testament makes the case for a continued, strategic, evangelistic focus to be essential in the life and ministry of the church.

The example of the early church serves as a model for churches today. Believers can receive power by the Holy Spirit of God to accomplish that task, and every believer has a role to play in the fulfillment of the mission. God has uniquely gifted each believer for advancing the gospel. While not all individuals have the gift of evangelism, each gift is part of the support structure for that mission.

The local church and her members, each utilizing their spiritual gifts, help advance the evangelistic mission. Those with the gift of teaching will teach others to obey all that Christ commanded. The pattern is to win converts, build them up in their faith, and send them out to win others. It is a cyclic proposition. If each one does his or her part and stays focused on the mission, the church continues to grow. In biblical terms:

> So Christ himself gave the apostles, the prophets, the evangelists, the pastors and teachers, to equip his people for works of service, so that the body of Christ may be built up until we all reach unity in the faith and in the knowledge of the Son of God and become mature, attaining to the whole measure of the fullness of Christ *(Ephesians 4:11-13).*

As churches became established, it became necessary for someone to provide direction to the local congregation in that great effort. That raises the question of spiritual authority within the local church or ministry, and who will lead them. Part of the difficulty faced by churches today is that their church polity diminishes the oversight function of those called into ministry. Power struggles, personal agendas, short tenures, mismatches between clergy and laity, as well as a whole host of other factors, seriously hinder the ability of the church body to function as designed. Such confusion has led to a great conflict of values between laity and clergy.

## Biblical Authority and Leadership

The impact upon evangelism has been staggering. Before bringing a serious strategy to bear upon a ministry context, the issue of biblical authority and leadership must be addressed. An organizational flow chart, a list of elders and deacons, and a thoughtful analysis are needed. Any serious effort will require leadership that empowers and guides the process. A lack of clear understanding here throws the entire project into danger. Christ led in His ministry. He trained leaders, equipped them, and empowered them to carry out His mission further. Leadership is critical. But a leader who has no one following is not leading. The attitude, passion, and willingness to serve as active followers is equally critical. Absent from many congregations today is the significant recognition of the priesthood or believers in the execution of key ministry roles

In one survey, 89 percent of church member respondents said, "The purpose of the church is to take care of my family's needs." The role of the pastor is to keep the sheep in the pen happy. Conversely, 90 percent of the pastors said the church was to win the world.[6] Therein lays a major part of the problem. Who shapes the evangelistic ministry of the church?

That role is the ordained, appointed elders who are tasked with leadership within the local churches. As such, they are primary leaders, with deacons serving in secondary leadership roles. Elders and deacons are no better than the other, but their functions are different.

Such was the practice of the early church: *"Paul and Barnabas appointed elders for them in each church and, with prayer and fasting, committed them to the Lord, in whom they had put their trust"* (Acts 14:23). Further instruction is provided in Acts 20:28, *"Keep watch over yourselves and all the flock of which the Holy Spirit has made you overseers. Be shepherds of the church of God, which he bought with his own blood."* And in 1 Peter 5:2 the Bible says: *"Be shepherds of God's flock that is under your care, watching over them—not because you must, but because you are willing, as God wants you to be; not pursuing dishonest gain, but eager to serve."*

Deacons serve to carry out that mission. The elders delegate the responsibility to participate in the mission to the deacons. It is necessary today to reassert the authority given to appointed overseers and for believers in general to commit themselves to honor that role for the sake of the gospel. It is critical to the mission that laity recognize the leadership of those called to serve as ordained elders, and follow them as they endeavor to follow Christ: *"Now we ask you, brothers and sisters, to acknowledge those who work hard among you, who care for you in the Lord and who admonish you"* (1 Thessalonians 5:12).

It seems likely that churches will enjoy only limited success until those issues find resolution. Some polities do not embrace this terminology and function with various forms of governance. Whichever polity exists within the church, there must be a recognition that leaders need to guide the evangelistic effort.

One might reasonably conclude from the preponderance of evidence noted in previous chapters, that many of today's churches have lost touch with the function of the Church as intended by God with respect to the call to evangelize. The examination of Old and New Testament evidence validates the point. With the theological evidence calling the Church to that purpose, and the understanding from others, the Church is not doing all it could to perpetuate evangelistic fervor.

The collective societal evidence provided speaking to the shift toward a postmodern mindset, illustrates the great gulf between the evangelistic fervor of the early church as conveyed in the biblical record, and the relative apathy of the modern church evidenced by steady decline and stagnant growth. The church today needs a reformation of mission.

The local church is to respond to the biblical and historical example and order their ministry, resources, time, and energy accordingly. There can be no clearer understanding of the role of the church than that of evangelism. Restoring humankind to a relationship with the Father is the central purpose of the gospel message. Each of the biblical accounts points to consistency in mission and purpose. There was a passion for the lost. It is the story of Christ's life and ministry, the apostles, and the early church.

Christ labored and sacrificed for the souls of all people. The apostles lived and ministered to carry out the great commission of Jesus Christ. From the beginning, the apostles preached and taught throughout their region of the world to draw all people to Jesus Christ. They did so at a great cost to themselves. Their zeal and unshakable commitment bore tremendous fruit as the church grew at a phenomenal rate. The church suffered persecution because of their devotion to Christ and the successes they had. Yet despite the persecution, they dispersed into various regions of the world, proclaiming the message of salvation. They formed churches, appointed elders, and continued the mission of spreading the gospel.

## Winning Converts

Down through the ages, winning converts was the central task of the church. The great commission of Christ gave very clear marching orders. The entirety of the New Testament biblical record offers a very clear understanding of the commands of Jesus Christ for His followers.

We would find it difficult to argue against the notion that the local church has a responsibility and a duty to be obedient to the commands of Christ and effectively evangelize the lost. That evangelistic effort is to encompass local evangelistic efforts as well as an active program to reach other people groups in distant lands. Failure to obey such clear directives is to be less than the church God desires. Yet this past century was marked by steady decline in churches both in the USA and abroad in most European nations.

Comparatively few churches in the USA are growing as a result of conversions. Transfer or negative growth has eclipsed conversion growth.

Many of the past and present theologians acknowledge the central task of the church is to evangelize the lost. At the same time, they acknowledge the relative ineffectiveness of the church today in accomplishing that task. The church must take seriously the commands of Christ in this area as much as in any other. Various authors have attempted to get the church back on track evangelistically, but with only marginal results taken together.

Many variables contribute to the lack of effectiveness in this critical area of the church. A church that desires to be biblical will indeed function evangelistically at a significant level. The measure of success is determined by those brought to Christ, equipped, and sent. The sending does not have to be on some mission field abroad. There is work to do in towns and cities across their own nation.

It is incumbent upon leadership within local churches today to assume their roles, commit themselves and their churches to be faithful to the evangelistic call, and prioritize accordingly. Future decisions must reflect that commitment.

There seems to be a disconnect between the theological call for focused Kingdom advancement and what happens in the local churches across the country. Evangelism is at the heart of Christian ministry. Most would agree with that philosophy outwardly, while some would wonder inwardly if it were true. It sounds good on a mission statement, but often seems too difficult to accomplish. Moving a church's systems and finances in alignment with an evangelistic emphasis can be a significant challenge.

The church exists to reach other people for Jesus Christ. In the past one hundred years, there have been a myriad of evangelistic efforts, strategies, and techniques developed and used. Those efforts range from the mass stadium evangelism of Billy Graham and others with a worldwide focus, to one-to-one approaches taught by Campus Crusade for Christ, for example. The impact on society from those efforts is not as significant as they could be. Patrick Johnstone and Jason Mandryk report, "The Christian Church is not impacting the nation as it should."[7]

To develop an integrative STEP system to evangelism, it is important to frame the initiative within the context of current issues facing local churches today. Johnstone and Mandryk suggest the spiritual heritage of the USA has eroded, due in part to humanism, New Age belief, and the homosexual agenda.[8] In more recent years, the rapid change of technology and its impact on the social fabric has radically changed the landscape. Numerous additional variables within the cultural fabric have had equal impact. While there are trends that challenge the traditional operating presuppositions of the local church in culture, much good has occurred through the cataclysmic shifts. However, the ability of the Church to anticipate and get in front of changes as a means by which its influence grows in culture, has not been what it could be.

There is still a critical and continued need for effective evangelism in every segment of society. Local churches need to make the Great Commission central to their church life, but only a fraction do. Again, much of the responsibility lies on the shoulder of the leader. Leaders need to understand more of the critical nuances of the culture and the implication for evangelistic strategies. The leader today needs to become a Christian leader.

## Cultural Communications

The Christian leader is a communicator who communicates within a particular context. The context is within a particular culture. The culture is the place in which the message either connects or does not connect. Culture is behavior, values, attitudes, beliefs, and expectations that a group shares and by which they live. Those values, attitudes, beliefs, and expectations shape the understanding of the collective. They are held in common and perpetuated by the collective.

Culture can be entrenched firmly or pliable in the face of significant effective pre-suppositional challenges. Social structures, practices, and decision making are informed by the greater cultural components. Culture functions as a guide to life decisions, purchases, governance, and industry. It is the collective will in both function and dysfunction.

Cultural fluency is an ability, coupled with a determination, which when paired with spiritual giftedness, aids in understanding as much about a particular culture as possible. The Christian leader is a student, interpreter of, and an expert in cultural trends at each level of the social fabric. That knowledge translates into strategic approaches to advance the Kingdom.

The prophetic voice is tied to understanding culture. The gospel message is relevant to and transformational in communication of truth born out of the depths of spiritual connectedness and informed by cultural understanding and application. It is made applicable in transformative ways through spiritual wisdom, ultimately tied to the presence of the Holy Spirit present within.

Christian Schwarz conducted a comprehensive study in the area of church growth. His research included information from over one thousand churches in thirty-two countries. The study, while considered flawed by some, nonetheless provides significant insight into the success of a church. The result of his massive study identified eight essential qualities that will ensure a churches growth if those qualities are developed. Needs-oriented evangelism is one of those factors and is relevant to our STEPs discussion. Schwarz states that:

> Hardly any aspect of church growth is as riddled with clichés, dogmas, and myths as the area of evangelism. This is true of those who view evangelism with skepticism as well as those who have made it their life long calling. Most discussions about this topic have blurred the distinction between methods of evangelism that may have been used successfully by one or many churches and true principles of evangelism, which may apply without exception to every church.[9]

The integration of the STEP system is innovative not because it develops a new method or the application of true evangelistic principles, but because it provides the framework for determining, which methods and principles are best in a specific application. Schwarz suggests further that approximately 10 percent of a congregation will have the gift of evangelism.[10] In addition to the 10 percent, others have a natural evangelistic bent or preferential style that can easily be determined. When discovered and used, many believers can be effective in evangelistic efforts. Every believer, regardless of giftedness, can be of service to evangelistic strategies in some connection. All have been called to make disciples. As a congregation places a strategic focus on its evangelistic effort, the church as a whole will benefit.

The point, Schwarz says, is to use existing relationships as points of contact for evangelism.[11] An existing relationship may have some commonality that provides a window of opportunity for the gospel to be shared. The STEP system places some emphasis on making those connections. It often seems that people feel pressured to develop friendships with non-Christians. The added pressure can make the relationship seem temporary, artificial, and strained. Some people can smell a set-up, however well-intentioned it may be. What may occur when people feel pressured to develop friendships with non-Christian people is a bait and switch situation that simply exploits the friendship. There may be a real absence of genuine and sincere concern for the person.

It is natural to build friendships on similar interests, hobbies, or activities. The common ground we share with another helps build credibility, acceptance, and continued contact. The trouble seems to be that many Christians separate their faith from their other interests. Shared interests are natural connecting points of evangelistic opportunity. There must be an increasing intentionality to existing relationships and methods of sharing the gospel in those circles. Those interests could be bridges to subcultures.

Most individuals have contact with another subculture through their interests, hobbies, or even vices. Each one represents a potential evangelistic opportunity. The STEP system was not designed to send people out into a field for which they have no connection or affinity. That would probably accomplish little.

Schwarz's *Natural Church* Development *Implementation Guide* asks an important question; "Are the forms and content of the evangelistic activities related to the needs of those you are trying to win?"[12] If they are not, then perhaps leaders are missing the mark.

Robert Logan and Thomas Clegg assert that, "We must learn to exegete our culture to discover the needs and mindsets which will indicate what would be Good News to these people."[13] They go on to say that today churches tend to be more culturally sensitive to the "foreign mission field" but forget to be culturally sensitive at home in the way church is done.[14] We might conclude that missionary support in some local churches may be higher because someone else is actually engaged in the process. Evangelistic activity on the home front is every bit as missional, but may lack some enthusiasm because it may require frontline attention.

The gap between the organizational culture of the church and the lifestyle of the unchurched seems to widen, particularly among those who lose sight of their mission. In an effort to be more culturally relevant to the unchurched, it is best to discern the target groups attitudes, interests, and needs by listening to people with God's heart and ears.[15]

Today the church is experiencing tremendous difficulty having a significant impact within the country, and the culture gap is widening. Reggie McNeal in his book *The Present Future,* writes, "The current church culture in North America is on life support. It is living off the work, money, and energy of previous generations from a previous world order."[16]

Many from previous generations, while they have accomplished much in the past, are reluctant to face the current cultural realities and reconfigure their ministries to address them. What they have developed over time is a brand of Christianity that more readily reflects the cultural values of a by-gone era, than the timeless values of Jesus. The central core of the message of Christ never changes. The methods and vehicles of communication must change to fit cultural realities and shifts.

McNeal further suggests, "The imminent demise under discussion is the collapse of the unique culture in North America that has come to be called 'church.' This church culture has become confused with biblical Christianity, both inside the church and out."[17]

Growth is relatively flat in the US among established churches, while gratefully, rapid growth occurs in other parts of the world. Only about 40-43 percent in America claim to go to church once each week. However, new evidence suggests that people were lying to pollsters and the actual number is closer 26 percent of

Americans. Those numbers tend to break down by generation with the builder generation, or those born before 1946[18] being the largest attendees while the rest are shrinking.[19]

The unchurched population is growing. The North American version of church is not influencing society as it once did. It is as if some have adopted a defensive posture, or hunker down mentality on the home front, rather than engaging this corner of the world offensively and aggressively with the gospel.

When the Church does engage, the greatest concentration of effort seems to be in the political arena in which Christian conservatives fight to keep morals and values from further erosion. Heavy involvement on that front without the balance of effective evangelistic strategies may diminish their effectiveness as redemptive agents. It may stir up resentment unnecessarily as well as foster a wrong view of what it means to be a Christian.

A guest speaker in a mainline denominational church in a small community challenged the audience to think outside the box evangelistically. If for no other reason than survival, they needed to become aggressive. The church had what they viewed as a problem, but was in fact an opportunity. Their parking lot had some curves, inclines, and declines that appealed to skateboarding kids. That was an opportunity. However, what they saw and acted on was a problem. They posted a "No Skateboarding Allowed on Church Property" sign in a prominent place in the parking lot. They had successfully defined their values, and communicated those to the children of the small community. They missed the opportunity to serve and minister. The following Sunday, that congregation was meeting to decide if they could or could not keep their doors open.

The questions become: What gospel are we communicating? Are the messages the church carries and the means by which it is carried, appealing to the unchurched? The conviction of Christians ought to be the gospel is the most attractive and beautiful message the church could communicate and people could ever hear. However, the world does not share that view. Perhaps some have botched the message up somewhere along the way—and what has often been communicated is not too far off from the pharisaical legalism that Jesus attacked. At least some of what passes for American Christianity is in need of reform.

Methodologies are in need of change. There is an approach in ministry that serves to withdraw from culture and build higher and thicker walls. McNeal writes, "Evangelism in this world view is about churching the un-churched, not connecting people to Jesus. It focuses on cleaning people up, changing their behavior so Christians (translation: church people) can be more comfortable around them. Refuge churches evidence enormous self-preoccupation. They deceive themselves into believing they are a potent force."[20]

Without a concerted effort of refocusing on the central mission, there will continue to be churches that will shut their doors. McNeal notes that an increasing number of people are leaving the institutional church to preserve their faith. Post congregational Christians are growing in number.[21]

Often times churches struggle to survive due to internal modes of thinking—outdated, out of touch with culture, naive, and myopic. It keeps them from a Kingdom focus. Some are preaching and teaching a brand of Christianity that is absent of the love and grace for one another and others that should characterize and define church. A not-so-subtle, self-righteous judgmentalism, which borders on arrogance, permeates church culture today.

Philip Yancey writes, "When asking airplane passengers about evangelical Christians, not once—not once—have I heard a description redolent of grace. Apparently that is not the aroma Christians give off in the world."[22]

As McNeal writes, "Absent a missiological center, North American theological reflections can easily drift toward figuring out who's right and whose wrong rather than who's going with the gospel, who's listening, and who's responding."[23]

Believers are not to adopt the worst of culture, but be salt and light in it. The Church is to use culture as a springboard for a greater message. There is a need to understand culture, engage it, and build connecting points to it to gain the hearing for the message churches proclaim. McNeal writes, "You cannot be faithful to the Great Commission without being culturally relevant." In addition,

"This reluctance to connect with the people outside the church is just further evidence the church in North America is a cultural phenomenon in America that is more about a particular religious culture than about Jesus or his mission."[24]

## Contagious Christianity

A point of conflict in many churches centers on music style and format. A wide variety of additional internal conflicts serve to undermine general effectiveness and create environments that are hostile to needed change. Change will come in one form or another, invited or not. Change will come despite any resistance to it. Change will result from pressures both inside and factors outside the church. If the church is to influence nations with the gospel, it must regroup and strategically confront the issues and challenges facing us.

*Contagious Christianity* is an evangelism curriculum designed by the staff of Willow Creek Church.[25] The curriculum was designed to be taught using video and a study guide. The program emphasizes the need for building relationships with non-churched people. Participants are encouraged to simply be themselves, understand their own spiritual story, develop a relationship with a pre-Christian, identifying the major points of the gospel message, introduce Christ into that relationship, share the gospel with them, and ask for a decision.

An essential element of the *Contagious Christian*[26] style is to know your own style. There are those with whom a relational approach just seems to fit. Others may gravitate to a more confrontational approach, while still others gravitate to an intellectual presentation. Most people ought to be comfortable enough with their own story to utilize the testimonial approach.

The average church member can invite someone to a special event. Volunteering is also a viable option, particularly with a younger generation who prefer to have some social welfare influence. The program encourages participants to discover their natural bent through a 36-question survey. Once their preference is determined, then each is given a brief overview of their own style.[27]

Participants are trained how to communicate the gospel through a simple illustration. As part of the training, there is one-to-one role-playing to help develop proficiency with the method. Each participant writes his or her life story—before Christ and after Christ. They then relate that story to one another in the context of a mock witnessing experience.

The designers of the Willow Creek evangelistic curriculum suggest the training be offered periodically, with refreshers for those who have been through the course. One of the chief areas of concern with evangelism is the lack of self-confidence in speaking to others about Christ. *Contagious Christianity* provides an easy-to-understand and use format that helps alleviate some anxiety about sharing. Anyone can do it after grasping the simple narrative.

The strengths of the approach are the relational aspect of the program. Everyone has a need to belong. The basic felt needs of an individual lend themselves to this type of approach. Most people have some connection with unchurched people. Edward Howell states that, "Loneliness is epidemic today and is the by-product of a society in which most people lack any substantial connection with someone who cares and listens attentively."[28]

Dick Staub, in his book *Too Christian Too Pagan*, identifies three problems he sees among believers today. Many Christians have no pagan friends. When they do, too many Christians befriend them only to convert them. They lack authenticity and sincerity. Those traits and that method run counter to the postmodern mindset. Many Christians do not influence their pagan friends.[29]

Willow Creek's Contagious *Christianity* builds on that reality and moves participants to establish interaction with them at a deeper, intentional level. The best way to reach people in today's culture seems to be connected to forming a positive relationship with them. That particular program is a low-pressure approach to evangelism.

The Willow Creek material provides an assessment tool to help the participant determine the evangelistic approach for which they are most suited. Mark Mittleberg breaks the approaches down into six categories of evangelistic approaches. Most people will identify with one or more of the following:

1. The confrontational approach
2. The intellectual approach
3. The testimonial
4. The interpersonal
5. The invitational
6. The service-oriented[30]

The Contagious Christianity study further encourages participants to look to their circle of influence, and connect with people they might ordinarily associate with in some way. A neighbor, co-worker, or relative are obvious examples.

While the Willow Creek approach seems to work exceptionally well, there are some weaknesses associated with its use. George Hunter identifies an important point relevant to relational evangelism that is critical to our understanding at this point. He states, "Establishment Christian leaders still take a dim view of pastors and churches who befriend pagans, sinners, and lost people who make apostolic outreach the priority of the church. Establishment Christianity always expects its people, pastors, and bishops care for, and fraternize with, church people."[31]

That fact poses a significant barrier to the program's effectiveness. Hunter's assessment should not be underestimated. Countless congregations strenuously resist ongoing contact with unchurched people beyond what is necessary for convenience and commerce. Those people tend to be judgmental and isolationist in disposition. It is not uncommon to hear a verbal rebuke from those who do not see the value or have neither the patience, tolerance, nor inclination to establish redemptive-focused relationships.

C. Peter Wagner attributed such attitudes to a more sinister culprit he identifies as the spirit of religion, which he defines as an "agent of Satan assigned to prevent change and to maintain the status quo by using religious devices."[32] He states further that in churches in which the spirit of religion thrives, people are "hesitant to risk the possibility of either losing control or losing money. So they capitulate to the religious spirit and do whatever it takes to preserve the status quo, while honestly thinking they are doing God's will."[33]

Many churches waited too long to change their way of thinking on that score. They tend to soften somewhat just before they exhale their last breath and the church fades into extinction. To help redefine the unchurched, leaders would do well to label people as "pre-Christian," putting the best possible and most hopeful spin on the situation.

Building relationships with pre-Christians does have a few additional down points. It often takes considerable time to reach a point where faith issues can be discussed without offending or jeopardizing the relationship. It is an approach that requires patience, tolerance, and grace. It may take many years before the relationship moves someone to faith, but it can be worth it. For instance, many have started by reaching children and often ended with the parents coming to faith as well. Relational evangelism is also an approach that requires a significant personal investment of time for uncertain results. The return on investment is not a sure thing.

There are many disappointments and hurts associated with reaching pre-Christians. Getting into the trenches costs the believer in energy, time, finances, and other relationships. Attempting to reach and have a positive influence in the lives of pre-Christian people can pose problems organizationally. While each individual is valued by God, people with a lack of vision, understanding, and grasp of what the role of the Church is in the world, may gravitate toward protectionism to safeguard their assets. At times, believers may place a higher priority on the institution of the church than the mission for which the Church exists. Often church budgets hold a veto power over mission. Additionally, when someone gets into the life of some pre-Christians, the sordid details associated with spiritual neglect can overwhelm even the earthiest of individuals.

It often takes tremendous time to move someone toward Christ, and calls for a high investment to evangelize friends and neighbors. Those who engage in the process must be strong enough not to be sucked into the complex and confusing lifestyles of those they are trying to evangelize.

Furthermore, it is common to suffer recrimination from fellow Christians who do not understand the approach and are often too quick to condemn. It is therefore expedient to keep pre-Christians from the established church where every bias, resentment, and stereotype can be reinforced until they are ready.

Wolfgang Simpson notes Willow Creeks' suggested sevenfold strategy of evangelism.

1. Spend quality time with non-Christians
2. Protect them from the church
3. Witness to those new friends about Jesus Christ
4. Protect them from the church
5. Lead them to Christ
6. Protect them from the church
7. When they have matured and are ready for culture shock, introduce them to the church from first time[34]

While some aspects of the strategy may appear negative, particularly items 2, 4, and 6, to Willow Creek it is simply an acknowledgment that churches are often hostile to people who are different either in appearance, attitude, or habit. Some of that hostility may be born out of the spirit of religion mentioned earlier.

Rick Joyner writes, "When the religious spirit succeeds in producing pride, it leads to perfectionism. The perfectionist person sees everything as black or white. This develops extremes, requiring that every person and every teaching be judged as either 100 percent right or 100 percent wrong. This is a standard that only Jesus could comply with."[35] There is a real threat from within that must be considered when attempting to reach people for Christ. The collective mentality or personality of a congregation can work either for or against an evangelistic effort.

It is ironic that some traditional churches present a significant obstacle to effective evangelism. It is important to the process to understand basic organizational dynamics. Churches are comprised of fallen people and therefore still subject to the common dynamics found among those who form organizational units. Having an awareness of how organizations tend to function and the dynamics involved that influence an outcome is exceptionally valuable information.

The seven-step process developed for this project reveals some of those dynamics and the extent of the disconnected nature of the traditional church with the central mission of the church. When believers have to consider questions of the churches' relevance, the Church as a whole is in a difficult position and must look realistically at the way "doing church" is accomplished.

There are not many additional weaknesses to this approach. Regardless of someone's particular evangelistic bent, the friendship model can be used in virtually any setting. The gospel can be shared in an understandable way at almost any time, anywhere. Leslie Newbigin writes,

> If the gospel is to be understood, if it is to be received as something that communicates truth about the real human condition, if it is, as we say, to 'make sense,' it has to be communicated in the language of those to whom it is addressed and has to be clothed in symbols which are meaningful to them.[36]

Contagious *Christianity* also helps participants understand the nature of those they will be dealing with. Some will be cynics, skeptics, indifferent, spectators, or those who are earnestly seeking. Suggested approaches are given for each particular personality type with questions that might be used in discussion with them. They also provide appropriate responses to the type of remarks that typically will arise from each personality type. In many ways, *Contagious Christianity* is consistent with one of the common approaches of Christ. He did not only speak to the crowd, but worked one to one on a very personal level. Friendship and relational evangelism is well suited to the postmodern mindset.

## The Alpha Course

Another effective evangelistic approach is the Alpha Course. Though this course is in part, relationally based, it is designed to touch the life of the average person on a level they can relate to and understand. The course is a result of the ministry of Nicky Gumbel of Holy Trinity Brompton Church in London, England. His course utilizes video format and a textbook format for adults and youth. He teaches the basic tenets of the Christian faith in an enjoyable and engaging presentation. The course discusses subjects such as: who Jesus is; why He died on the cross; how to be sure of your faith; why and how to pray; who the Holy Spirit is, etc. In Gumbel's experience, the postmodern mind will ordinarily not accept a dogmatic presentation of the gospel that fails to invite or encourage honest discussion and a freedom to raise questions.

It matters tremendously how the gospel is presented. Today, people desire something that is authentic and real. They can spot a fake and will reject an overly authoritative posture in presentation. Gumbel has honed his presentation skills to a very effective degree. His style is consistent with the three principles of communication given by Aristotle: intelligence, character, and good will.[37] While it is possible to go through the course without the video resource, Gumbel's information and presentation are persuasive tools. Presentation makes all the difference in the world.

The Alpha Course presents the gospel in a way that reflects the cultural realities of the day. A growing number of people in the USA culture are ignorant of the basic elements of Christianity. The dominate source of their information comes from television sources, some of which leave a questionable impression.

There is a real disconnect between pre-Christian people and their basic level of understanding of Christianity. It is common to run across people who have no understanding of church life, or even a general familiarization with the stories of the Bible. That is a huge transition from the culture of the last century.

The strengths of the Alpha Course are numerous. It has a relational component that is a definite strength. It does not rely upon that, however, as much as it does the content of the information presented. Alpha groups are encouraged to meet in homes once a week. The host prepares a meal for the members of the group. The group is comprised of a mixture of Christians and pre-Christians. The pre-Christians are invited to participate with the rest of the group for a period of about ten weeks.

The format shifts to a retreat setting when the course begins to deal with the Holy Spirit. The retreat setting is the optimal choice. However, some participants found that pre-Christians do not want to leave the safety and numbers of the original group, and resist the notion of a retreat in another location. Since the purpose of the course is to reach pre-Christians, failing to accommodate that target group could diminish the results.

Each group will share a meal, converse, get to know one another, watch a video presentation, fill out a workbook, and discuss the topic of the evening. The Alpha Course is designed to provide a forum for frank, open discussions about Christianity.

The Alpha Course material is evangelical and doctrinally sound. It is also entertaining and intellectually challenging. People with no background in the church will respond positively to it, should they have the opportunity. George Hunter notes that Alpha leaders observe that through the Alpha experience, seekers are partially socialized into the Christian belief, and the small group experience is indispensable in the socialization process. A group leader functions essentially as a host and conversation facilitator, rather than a speaker or teacher, and the seekers are treated like guests rather than auditors or pupils. Within several weeks, the group leader has developed pastoral care relationship group members—encouraging people, praying for people, praying with people, inviting (without pressure) responsive to the Holy Spirit. Each week, group members ask their questions, and express their ideas and feelings and discuss Christianity's possibilities for their lives.[38]

The course is not without some weaknesses. One such weakness is the level of commitment that is required to complete it. While it can be delivered in a number of different formats, the Alpha home meeting method mentioned is preferable. The high level of commitment is an obstacle. Because of the number of weeks that it takes to complete the course, there are tremendous sacrifices that must be made by the participants. The host and hostess has their home life interrupted for several weeks. There is a cost associated with meals, drinks, and the like. While those costs can be shared, it is nonetheless an expense. If the right group of Christians is not a part of the course, dysfunctions may manifest and discourage pre-Christian participants.

The book is based upon case study experience. When the course curriculum was field tested, some participants complained about the stress of participating in one more activity. On occasion, the pre-Christians would invent reasons for not attending. If they begin to be convicted but would rather not change, they may flee. The fact that it takes so long to go through limits the types of people who will most likely participate. They will be people who are indeed seeking something. Those who may be tepid in their interest will most likely bolt before the course is complete. The effort should be undergirded with prayer.

Overall, the course is good. If the weaknesses can be addressed in a way that does not water it down yet still achieves its intended purpose, it would be great.

## Evangelism Explosion

*Evangelism* Explosion by D. James Kennedy was a tool used widely in the 1970s and early 1980s as a tool for training laymen for evangelism. It consisted of memorizing Scripture and a gospel presentation that could be shared with individuals, ultimately leading them to a decision to receive Christ. It had great success initially and over a period of years. However, its effectiveness began to wane as shifts in society began to occur.[39]

Of the evangelistic programs, *Evangelism Explosion* could be considered a hard sell. It is an aggressive approach that moves believers to present the gospel to prospective Christians, and get them to make a decision. One section suggests that believers "use judo technique" in handling objections raised to Christianity.[40] It worked in a time when certain religious assumptions on the authority of Scripture, the role of the Church, and base-level knowledge of Heaven and hell were part of the fabric of the culture. Those factors helped the approach have a greater level of success. Today, so much has changed in the social fabric of the nation that some cultural presuppositions relevant to Christian belief no longer exist.

The strength of the approach is the direct nature of the presentation. It is well suited to certain situations. However, there are some weaknesses. Establishing relationships and earning the right to be heard was not part of the strategy. It seemed to work on a funnel philosophy. Present it to as many people as you can;

some will enter the funnel and some will not. Today, people tend to shy away from positions that are stated dogmatically without addressing questions or underlying assumptions.

The USA is a pluralistic society in which the Bible is no longer viewed by the public as being authoritative above any other sacred book. Churches can no longer expect to have Christian claims accepted broadly. Leslie Newbigin remarks upon a current cultural reality when he notes the attitude of universal doubt that suggests, "Every belief should be doubted until it could be validated by evidence and arguments not open to doubt."[41]

He also states, "Pluralism is conceived to be a proper characteristic of secular society, a society in which there is no officially approved pattern of belief or conduct. It is therefore also conceived to be free society, a society not controlled by accepted dogma but characterized rather by the critical spirit which is ready to subject all dogmas to critical and even skeptical examination."[42]

That is the culture today.

While Evangelism *Explosion* may have been used tremendously at one point in history, its use and acceptance today is not nearly as broad or as successful. The primary weaknesses are the direct dogmatic approach seems offensive to many people. It also demonstrates a lack of sensitivity to current cultural realities.

For the church to be effective again and specifically become effective in reaching people for Jesus Christ, it is essential to understand the realities of the world in which the church and her people live. In a pluralistic society, the Christian worldview no longer can be assumed to have any basic level of acceptance among the general populace.

Many people in the USA have no understanding of Christian ideas or concepts and the name of Christ is nothing more than a swear word. Leonard Sweet writes, "The challenge of leadership today is to call people to a moral and spiritual way of looking at and being in the world when that world itself has developed a whole new way of being and thinking."[43]

Using the metaphor of the naturalization process, Sweet further suggests that people are either natives or immigrants in this new world. Immigrants are defined as having been born before 1962, and natives as having been born after that date. Immigrants are as foreigners in a strange land. The world as it was in previous generations changed rapidly. The rate of change is phenomenal with no signs of slowing down.

The ability of the Church to function meaningfully in a "www" world of nearly 1 billion websites strong, which moves at the speed of a button click, will be determined by the response to the new realities. The world, and new ways of understanding and closing the gap between cultures, exists when the Church most needs new inroads to hearts. The Church, which seems always to adjust slowly, may become increasingly ineffective as a social change agent if it does not aggressively respond to cultural realities in a positive way that enables the message to go forward.

## Casual Spirituality

Part of the reason for decline in cultural impact in the US, is due to a casual spirituality that expects little of its adherents and perpetuates systems that fail to deploy followers to passionate spirituality in the marketplace.

The effective strategy must be born out of a solid understanding of culture. Society, whether we like it or not, is an integration of a wide variety of interests, activities and life philosophies. Some of those interests and activities are in direct conflict with one another, and some function only on the periphery and outside the general knowledge of the populace. There is a collective will operant in any society. That will, or personality, is reflected in the culture and belies the extent to which a comprehensive, cohesive understanding exists and the degree to which strategic, integrated approaches to evangelism can be successfully brought to bear on the whole.

Christian leaders, within the context of a local church, must make themselves aware of the culture at all levels, and as deeply as is possible. One must bring to bear the collective insights from cultural practitioners. Christian leaders step into the arena and go where others will not. As stated previously, they are ready for the fight, fighting with spiritual tools; and at strategic times using the tools of the world. The Christian leader realizes that while we fight against principalities and powers, the battle is often played out and manifested in society, right before our eyes. Too often, we have grown callused and removed from the brutality of the battle.

The US American culture has a myriad of alternative worldviews that are prevalent among those in our pews.[44] George Barna writes that "A sizable segment (one-seventh) responded that their religious beliefs differ significantly from those of the church crowd."[45] After September 11, 2001, Islam has been the subject of much discussion. Islamic groups have exploited the dialogue, some to their advantage. There is a resurgence of Eastern thought in American society. The Dali Lama has a best seller. Feng Shui, which is repackaged Buddhism, is gaining popularity as a consideration in home décor. Yoga and tai-chi are being practiced and encouraged in hospitals. A group of scientists who believe the government has bred with aliens make national news with the announcement that they will clone a human. "The Force" is no longer just a nondescript movie name for power in a *Star Wars* movie, but a new religion practiced by *Star War* fans.

The smart phone literally opens up the world to immediate access of information. Radio has gone satellite. Walmart now serves as a distribution point for the service. So much is occurring in the world and in culture that it is difficult to keep up.

Perhaps one of the most significant aspects of cultural shift is that there is no longer a set of characteristics that can define USA culture. Baseball, hotdogs, apple pie, and Chevrolet are not accurate descriptors anymore. America is an exceptionally diverse nation made up of a variety of different types of people and nationalities from all around the world. It is not the monolithic culture that many thought it to be at one time. Just about anywhere one travels now, English and Spanish can be found side by side on products, public buildings, and government documents.

The notion that the country is a "melting pot" where various people groups come and assimilate into the fabric of the American culture does not accurately describe the country today. Instead, the USA is growing into a multicolored, multiethnic collection of subcultures. Some of those subcultures are not defined by ordinary definitions of race or national origin, but by lifestyle affinities. Each subculture has its own traits, likes and dislikes, characteristics, attributes, and in some cases, even language.

## Reaching "Postmoderns"

If the church hopes to have a broad-based impact with the gospel of Jesus Christ in this culture and in this country, leaders must understand that the approach must address the cultural diversity within the country. In order to reach each subculture effectively, it is incumbent upon believers to labor to understand their unique qualities and design strategic initiatives that will be effective in those specific subcultures.

The church cannot adopt one form of evangelism and simply hope it does the job, and then wonder in amazement when it does not. One cultural group may respond well to event-oriented approaches. Another group may respond well to a direct street evangelism approach; another group may respond well to an activity that they share or have in common. Each subculture is reachable if churches are willing to take the time and investigate the best course of action for any given scenario.

The message never changes; but how that message is delivered and the means by which it is delivered must always be under constant review. Leaders often decry a cookie cutter approach to church structure, design, or programming. It is essential to understand that there is no overarching cookie cutter approach to evangelism. There was a time when the Billy Graham Crusades represented the major thrust of evangelistic efforts within the nation. That time may well have passed. It may come around and be successful again in later years.

There may have been a time and may still be a time when a direct, confrontational, high-pressure approach is needed and would result in the greatest number of conversions. But, it seems the best approach for today's culture is a relational style, a softer sell that can be molded to fit into a number of scenarios. And there will be many, not only because America is a pluralistic society, but because of the strong postmodern bent the culture has taken.

The influence of postmodernism on society affects the strategies that can be employed evangelistically. Graham Johnston, in his book *Preaching to a Postmodern World,* suggests that ten distinctives have emerged culturally and those distinctives alter the way in which we communicate the message.[46]

Many people are reacting to modernity and all its tenets. Objective truth is rejected along with a certain social skepticism and suspicion of authority. Those characteristics alone aid in weakening the social underpinnings. The postmodern is like someone on a "missing persons" list in search of a self and an identity. Morality is blurred, and whatever is expedient is accepted. Postmoderns continue to search for the transcendent. They live in a media-driven world unlike any previous. A wide variety of products are marketed to postmoderns in quick, fast-paced, rapidly-changing formats. They will engage in the knowing smirk, and are in pursuit of something real and authentic. That sentiment is reflected in the lyrics of one of the culture's most influential rock groups, Coldplay. A lyric in one of their most popular early songs belts out the refrain, "Give me real, don't give me fake!"

Postmoderns are on a quest for community. They want to belong and feel needed. Theirs is a material world.[47] In response to the influence of the postmodern mind on the work of the church, Brian McLaren asserts that the church must engage the culture as it is.[48] He suggests fifteen ideas for maximizing opportunities in the postmodern world. Chief among them is distinguishing between genuine Christianity and the individual and various culture-encoded versions of it.

Under critical scrutiny, someone may be easily convinced that what passes for the church is an Americanized version that erects both subtle and not so subtle tests of spiritual fitness, legalism, judgmentalism, and an overwhelming lack of grace. Those who do not match up or fit the mold are encouraged to continue their involvement elsewhere or are marginalized where they are.

We should see truth and goodness where they exist in postmodernism by seeking common ground, as well as magnifying the importance of faith personally and for society as a whole. The church must also be fairer. By that McLaren means, "we need to be more careful about applying a degree of scrutiny to other (other Christians, non-Christians, postmoderns, the world, mega churches, or whomever) that we ourselves cannot withstand."[49]

Believers are part of an experiential culture. Churches need to be creatively embracing the experiential hunger that is so evident in society. It is also up to church leadership to address the postmoderns' existential predicament, understand their stories, communicate their own, and not be fearful of addressing any subject. There is also a not-so-subtle coercion and pressure that some tend to utilize that seems to push people further away. The absence or presence of those coercive elements may be closely related to people's theological assumptions.

Viewing postmodernism as a real part of the culture is important. Postmoderns are in churches, workplaces, homes, and schools. Churches must further rely on art, music, literature, and drama to communicate the gospel message, while believing that the Holy Spirit is out there at work already. Believers must become seekers again, reassert the value of community and rekindle the experience of it.[50]

The influence of the postmodern mind on culture is profound. The implications for ministry in particular and evangelism specifically, require leaders to think differently about what and how believers do to influence society for Christ. There are always those who are skeptical about shifts in how a local church functions. There are always those who do not understand the times, and others who hold a naive view of the challenges before the Church. Not surprisingly, some of those apprehensions may arise from generational mindsets that are at odds with one another. However, apprehensions aside, it cannot be denied that there is a great need for evangelism, and evangelism that is mindful of its audience.

## Updating Efforts

Barna reports there are an estimated ninety-five to one hundred million Americans who are unchurched.[51] He states that an important revelation of his research has been that unchurched people are not "people persons." "They tend to be more combative, less rational, lonelier, and less flexible."[52] They are aggressive, energetic, driven people who do not attend church because it is not worth their time and effort. They are more likely to respond to a personal invitation rather than pressure. They may resist polished marketing efforts and are generally skeptical about institutions, especially slick religiosity.[53] Those characteristics and traits pose a significant challenge as well to the evangelistic efforts of the local church.

The reality is that some evangelistic methods have proven exceptionally effective in their time, but today are proving to be significantly less impactful. For instance, at events such as annual revival weeks, the stated expectation is that converts would be won through the evangelistic revivals. What most often occurs: limited effort in advertising; attendance primarily by those who would attend any time the doors were open; lack of effort to invite unchurched people (who probably would not attend anyway, depending on age group); a lack of young people in attendance; and a tepid response from those in attendance. Often, it seems that the church's resources could be used a bit more effectively with another strategy.

There are still a few strategies that have proven effective in communicating the gospel. Many, however, need to be evaluated to determine their continued viability given new cultural realities and the postmodern mind. The influence of a postmodern mind ripples through the layers of the cultural social fabric. The tendency now to put all world religions on equal par, or even superior to Christianity for that matter, changes the underlying social assumptions by which leaders operate. Spirituality can be anything and nothing. Syncretistic views—the fusion of different forms of belief or practice—are becoming more prevalent. Some evangelism strategies may need to be adapted, changed, or dropped if a sincere desire exists to truly commit to impacting the current culture with Christianity.

Brian McLaren, in his book *Church on the Other Side,* designed a matrix for dealing with the postmodern mind. He suggests that believers have to understand in order to connect. As such, churches should look for the positives within the postmodern mindset, have an appropriate humility, understand and appreciate a healthy skepticism, realize that there is still a thirst for spirituality, openness to faith, a degree of tolerance, and a limited relativism.[54]

Street preaching was an effective evangelistic tool at one time. Tent revivals were once well attended. Camp meetings were evangelistic powerhouses in earlier times. Church revival services used to be the means by which people came to Christ. Today, each one of those methods has faded in the ability to serve as strong evangelistic vehicles. Today, the revival service has become the spiritual emphasis series where the old faithful gather to hear how bad it is out there. The Billy Graham stadium events have been filled largely with Christians. That is not to say that they are no longer effective, but does suggest that they are not nearly as effective as they once were.

The USA has experienced sharp cultural shifts in the past 40 to 50 years that have made many of the traditional approaches less appealing and less effective. It is time, given the cultural makeup, to adjust to the social and cultural shifts and create new innovative and strategic approaches that will work in this present age.

George Barna suggests that restoring evangelistic power in churches is a monumental challenge. He notes that significant obstacles to effective evangelism exist within the church. The absence of prayer is most notable. Barna suggests that some churches do not "own" the outreach as the centerpiece of its purpose. He states, "If your church has not made evangelism the centerpiece of its ministry, get on your knees and pray for forgiveness from God as well as for wisdom on how to reinvigorate the church so that it is evangelistic in nature."[55]

George Hunter writes that the church today is confronted with the same cultural environment in which the early church began to grow. He defines the age as the new apostolic age and suggests that leaders are facing a population with no knowledge of the gospel, in which the state is hostile to the Church and confronted with other entrenched religions. It is within that culture that an invitation to join the Christian faith is extended.[56]

Hunter notes further that effective apostolic congregations tend to take the following steps. The congregation will research the community and the unchurched population. They will find all relevant facts to guide them in decision making. They profile their target population and develop a clear mission and plan that fits the profile. A strategy is developed for reaching unchurched people, which includes training and deploying their people into the work. People will be challenged to commit their lives. Their worship will reflect seeker sensitivity and open them up for an encounter with God. From that point on, an effective apostolic congregation will enlist the involvement of other congregations.[57]

Some churches may have a significant grasp of cultural nuances, but that cannot be said about many. Churches are simply not effective at understanding social trends and capitalizing on them. Business and industry, particularly those that rely on consumer behavior, on the other hand, invest significant resources into understanding specific markets to maximize their market share in target demographics. Because their economic survival depends on information about their market, many have become effective at communicating to the subcultures to which they wish to bring their product.

Church leaderships are only marginally aware of the vast nuances in the wide array of consumer markets. However, it does not have to stay that way. The local church can once again be effective in its own back yard. To accomplish that end, a local body needs to strategically gather information about their target audience and determine the best approach for that specific market. One of the biggest obstacles is the mindset that suggests outreach activity ends with the integration of people into the local church.

Holding a tent revival for a group of motorcycle enthusiasts at "Bike Week" in Wildwood, New Jersey, may not prove to be an effective strategy given the dynamics of that subculture. Going door to door with the "Four Spiritual Laws" in some neighborhoods may prove more harmful than good. A citywide evangelistic crusade may attract more churched than unchurched people. Efforts to develop relationships with people with whom one shares no common ground may only lead to greater frustration, resentment toward Christians and a sense of failure and guilt for the faithful.

## The "Experience" Outreach

A recent evangelism strategy was implemented in a community aimed at reaching the lost. Community churches came together and committees were formed. Churches were involved for months in planning, raising funds, and making prayerful preparation.

Well-known national performers were lined up to take part and advertisements began. Signs were placed all over the area. From the inside, it would look like every avenue had been used to promote the event. Looking at the advertising from the point of view of an unchurched person, one would not have any idea about what the event was. Worse yet, it appeared as if it were marketed to a churched audience.

In the end, the results were nothing like the planners expected. Believers enjoyed the entertainment and good messages in the week-long effort, but the conversions were not proportional to the effort and significantly fell short of expectations. They did not do their homework. Good intentions do not always bear good results.

These approaches are not in themselves wrong. They may have worked at particular times in a particular way. They may yet be effective in some context. The question is not so much the methodology but an issue of choosing the best methodology for the right situation at the proper time and right place for the intended group. To establish which approach is most effective, significant work must be accomplished.

Some of those within the business community seem to understand the diversified nature of the American culture. Industries tend to flourish when they understand cultural variances and adapt their products or services to meet the needs and demands of the often-shifting market. It seems as if the church fails to understand the culture as well as businesses do.

The objective of most successful businesses is to increase shareholder wealth. To accomplish their objective, they must understand the markets, the competition, and the culture in which they do business. Their economic and business survival depends on attention to those factors. Those that do it best tend to gain greater market share. Those that fail to pay attention to the cultural changes tend to flounder at best, and at worst, lose their competitive edge and position in the market before they finally slip into oblivion.

Joseph Pine and James Gilmore note in their book, *The Experience Economy*, that a pound of coffee that may sell for the equivalent of ten cents a cup on the future's market (depending on supply and demand), may translate into a two to five-dollar cup of coffee in a five-star restaurant. Moving a consumer to that price level for a very inexpensive product signifies the perceptive nature of the business owner, who then enjoys the greater profit margin. The whole premise of their book is that culture has changed significantly enough that if a business fails to realize that *people pursue experiences,* they may no longer maintain their competitive edge in the marketplace. The five-dollar coffee cup is not really about the taste of the coffee. The five star restaurants and the experience in them add value to a commonly inexpensive product.[58]

Simply being aware of people's preferences, needs, and desires can alter the way the gospel is communicated and subsequently received. The methodologies that can be applied evangelistically may also be altered. To ignore the wide array of critical factors within groups, individuals, or subcultures jeopardizes the opportunity to influence them.

Some questions should pose to the participants as a way to prepare them for Step Two, where they will work on researching these factors among the groups to which they want to minister. Their responses can demonstrate potential connecting points. Too often people lose heart or have a negative view of evangelistic efforts because it requires them to move so far out of their comfort zone. Some evangelistic strategies will require that, some will not.

Opportunities that exist within an individual's existing likes and dislikes will most likely result in greater enthusiasm, a positive attitude, and potential short-term gains. Participants should be asked to consider these questions:

- In what hobbies, interests, organizations, or groups do you have an interest?
- How do you invest your time and resources into the hobby, interest, or group?
- What potential points of contact are within your area of interest?
- Of those groups, what is the percentage of non-Christian, unchurched, or de-churched people with whom you associate?

- How could your interests, hobbies, organizations, or groups, serve as evangelistic entry points?
- What potential problems do you see?
- How can potential problems be overcome?

These types of questions focus on the same type of "market research" and planning that businesses use to be effective. Some might argue that some churches are already driven by commercial considerations. In some cases, that may be true. However, in evangelistic efforts, knowing the mind and heart of the people to whom the gospel is communicated makes sense, saves time, and may prevent wasted effort and frustration. The strategic and integrative approach can help accomplish that.

My college marketing class featured a constantly stated and tested definition of marketing. In that class, marketing has been defined as the "total system of [interactive] business activities designed to plan, price, promote and distribute want-satisfying products to target markets to achieve organizational objectives." That definition has profound implications not only for business activities, but the church as well. The business that successfully plans, promotes, and positions their products or services within a target market based on a thorough knowledge of the culture in which they do business, will enjoy continued profits for its wisdom.

The distribution mechanism matters as well. For greater effectiveness, it makes sense to equip believers and engage them as the principle means through which a saving knowledge of Jesus Christ is brought to market. Today, however, there is a sense that the pastoral leadership is the principle means. That is not effective, as years of decline in the USA attests. *Our emphasis on pastoral leadership without the corresponding balance of focus on the priesthood of believers decreases our opportunity.*

The same principles apply to the church when determining evangelistic strategies. Church and ministry leaders, too, need to have a better grasp of what is occurring culturally, plan strategically for it, and strongly promote the gospel to targeted audiences. Simply wringing the hands and decrying the negative shifts church leaders do not appreciate will do little toward moving the church closer to effectiveness in evangelistic efforts. The mission to the world is to communicate a message that is life changing. It matters how that is accomplished.

## Church "Business"

Fastcompany.com is an Internet site that offers information to businesses that can help them competitively. The tone and message of Fast Company stands in stark contrast to the approach churches tend to take. The name implies a philosophy of business that emphasizes the need for corporations to be in a position to change or adapt rapidly to shifts in society or in demand for products. An article asks the question, "Is Your Company Up to Speed?"[59] They were emphasizing the need for companies to be committed to creating new leaders, launching new products, and building the organization for speed. The site also provides questions that help evaluate a company's performance and provides updates on the fastest growing companies.

The business leader's approach recognizes the need for speed in a competitive marketplace. They assert that business and industry must understand and interpret cultural shifts and changes at a much quicker rate than in virtually any other area or segment of society. The church, on the other hand, seems to routinely be fifteen to twenty years behind cultural shifts. All across the landscape, churches are changing gradually. To call the style of worship in many churches "contemporary worship" is a misnomer. By the time a number of churches have initiated "contemporary worship" services, the emerging church with its emphasis on being "cutting edge" has already reformatted how they do church. By the time churches initiate something that is acceptable to one segment of culture, we are ignoring other segments that have moved beyond that point.

The fastcompany.com site is incredibly time sensitive and connects current, relevant issues of importance to the business community and the nation at large. The page has an admonition for the business community. Business is challenged to be aware of the need for quick adjustments to social changes in order to maximize profits. That is accomplished by listening to stockholders, evaluating, and adjusting strategies accordingly. The local church needs to adopt a similar philosophical approach if it desires to achieve greater evangelistic effectiveness. In the case of the church, however, the stockholders are not those already in the fold—they are people who will not become part of the fold because evangelistic strategies are weak or the church appears irrelevant.

The Church should realize that some successes within the business community are due in part to their awareness of key social factors that are important and reflect an understanding of trends in current culture. Any church would do well to embrace culturally significant issues as a way to more effectively communicate the gospel in today's culture.

The reality is that people invest thousands of dollars in subculture and interest-related events, clothing, books, magazines, hobbies, and the like. Those points of interest represent an opportunity to the church that they may not have seized upon strategically. There is no good reason for church leaders to be unaware of the ever-changing nuances of culture. There have always been people who view the church as an agent of redemption in the world and those outside the church must come to understand, accept, and embrace. Nevertheless, the church will not be as effective as it might be if it understood better the field in which it labors.

## Closing the Gap

Fastcompany.com frequently features articles about the need for businesses to have the internal culture of change so that they may quickly make adjustments in response to or in front of shifting trends.[60] The church can be equally adept at rapid change provided a commitment to effectively communicating the message takes a higher priority than institutionalized, but ineffective, strategies. As it is, there seems to be a ten to twenty-year gap between the adjustments within culture and the ability of some churches to respond. Even within churches that are considered "cutting-edge," there seems to be an inability to shift quickly enough with the cultural changes. That consideration may translate into an inability to facilitate a more effective communication of the gospel. What works in one-time period and in one culture may prove ineffective in the next.

Additionally, some argue that it is not the place of the church to shift with the ever-changing winds of culture. The church's role is to be the standard against which cultural shifts are measured and either embraced or corrected. However, such an approach aids in creating a view of the church as disconnected and out of touch. Battling that view only makes the need for cultural impact that much harder to achieve.

Culture is continually changing. Companies that offer products or services for which there is no constant demand must stay on top of the various nuances of social change in order to position themselves and their product for success in a competitive marketplace. John P. Kotter states, "The rate of change is not going to slow down any time soon. If anything, competition in most industries will probably speed up even more in the next few decades."[61]

Due to the presence of a particular mindset about what evangelism is in the mind of the average believer, an environment of change has to be developed. Change is not something many churches are good at or readily embrace. The local church must realize that change is constant. Society is rarely stagnant. In order to influence culture, church leaders must be students of society and be willing to adapt the message and methodologies accordingly. As Spencer Johnson writes in *Who Moved My Cheese*, "Change happens, they keep moving the cheese, anticipate change, monitor change, adapt to change quickly, change, enjoy change, be ready to change quickly and enjoy it again and again."[62]

To guide the process and change the way a church looks at and executes the evangelistic task, an eight-stage process for change, developed by John P. Kotter and described in his book *Leading Change*, was considered when writing this book, *Moving the Church in Seven STEPs*. He outlined a systematic approach to advance an organization forward. That outline is applicable to the system of a local church and can help move them toward missional effectiveness. Kotter first suggests an organization should establish a sense of urgency by examining the market and competitive realities and identifying and discussing crisis, potential crisis, or major opportunities.[63]

Second, Kotter suggests creating a guiding coalition by putting together a group with enough power to lead the change and get the group to work together like a team. Third, develop a vision and a strategy that will help direct the change effort, and developing strategies for achieving that vision. Fourth, an organization must communicate the change vision using every vehicle possible to constantly communicate the new vision and strategies, and have a guiding coalition role model the behavior expected.

The organization must next empower a broad-based action by getting rid of obstacles and changing systems or structures that undermine that change vision along with encouraging risk taking and nontraditional ideas, activities, and actions. Sixth, generate short-term wins through planning for visible improvements in performance, or "wins," creating those wins, and visibly recognizing and rewarding people who made the wins possible.

Seventh, consolidate gains and produce more change by using increased credibility to change all systems, structures, and policies that do not fit together and do not fit the transformation vision; hiring, promoting, and developing people who can implement change vision; and reinvigorating the process with new projects, themes, and change agents.

Last, the organization should work to anchor new approaches in the culture by creating better performance through customer, productivity oriented behavior, better leadership, more effective management, articulating the connections between new behaviors and organizational success, and developing means to ensure leadership development and succession.[64]

J. Stewart Black and Hal B. Gregersen offer a four-step process to lead an organization toward greater effectiveness. They suggest that an organization do the right thing and do it well, discover the right thing is now the wrong thing, do the right thing but do it poorly at first, eventually do the right thing well.[65] Some of what they suggest parallels Kotter's process.

Clayton Christensen[66] suggests that: first, an organization starts before they need to. The underlying principle is that too often organizations wait too long to make needed changes. It seems as if some churches decide to make changes in their strategy when the problem they hope to address has already reached critical mass. An area church made a decision to be evangelistically oriented in their neighborhood. They were motivated by the realization that if they did not act to increase church attendance, they might have to close. There were two important points they neglected to consider. To begin, their motivation for evangelism was based on their immediate survival rather than a true commitment to communicating the gospel. Additionally, the strategy they used would appeal only to Christians. The effort failed to accomplish the desired result.

A sense of urgency is also important—Kotter and Christensen share that identified need. If that is true and recognized by business leaders, how much more important is the mission of communicating the good news of Christ? It too is urgent. The strategic and integrative approach to evangelism works to ensure the right people in the right place leading the right strategy.

Additionally, Kotter suggests creating a team and a process for shaping ideas. He concludes by identifying the need to "train the troops" to identify ideas that improve the organization's position.[67] In the book, *Execution,* authors Larry Bossidy and Ram Charan state that the strategy process defines where an organization wants to go, the people process defines who is going to get it there, and the operating plan provides the path.[68]

Michael Slaughter in *Unlearning Church,* suggests that there is great power behind innovation and change: A culture that seeks to fill the spiritual vacuum left by scientific materialism can easily become unbalanced in its quest. Unlearning churches keep the focus on human worth, health, and personal relationships. The result is this: Unlearning churches are incredible atmospheres of innovation and change.[69] One must choose between fear or faith.

Mark Divine of Seal Fit, writes:

The wolf of love and courage resides in the heart. The wolf of fear resides in the mind. The wolf that gets fed the most is the strongest and dominates our being. The wolf of fear is the most active and hungry, eager to trick us into thinking he is the most important wolf. The wolf of love and courage, on the other hand, is docile, loving and generous. He will take a back seat to the wolf of fear because he deplores conflict." Both wolves are an integral part of us of course. We can't kill the wolf of fear and hating him is the same as feeding him. We should strive to control the wolf of fear – to tame him by re-directing fear energy into assertiveness and discipline.

Meanwhile, we should strive to feed the wolf of love and courage. Feeding the wolf of love and courage makes us more kind, patient, tolerant, powerful and present. We will avoid conflict and be better leaders. We won't hesitate to lean into the hard tasks; fear will cease being an influence in our lives. The nice thing is that by feeding the wolf of love and courage we will be simultaneously taming the wolf of fear.[70]

## Evangelism as a Battleground

The Church—as imperfect as the whole body of believers is—is the vessel through which God chooses to bring the message of salvation. Chapter Two included insights from Christian leaders about the condition of the Church today and its effectiveness in communicating its message, what needs to be accomplished to strike a chord with the culture, some existing methods that are used today, and the need to select the best possible methods for focused impact.

The methods by which the gospel is proclaimed must reflect an understanding of the cultural nuances that exist at present, how they continually shift over time, and how they dominate the landscape. The Church must be culturally well informed and able to adapt rapidly to societal shifts. Each failure to adjust makes evangelistic efforts more difficult.

It is clear also that the Scriptures point to the need for an evangelistic fervor. Historically, the Church and her critics from within have noted the need to reach people with the good news and the apparent lack of effectiveness in accomplishing that.

Jesus was strategic in His ministry. Paul and the apostles were strategic in their ministries. The Church must also be strategic. The intervention focused on in this book:

- Brought components into the local church that guided them toward thinking strategically
- Focused on real opportunities that lie dormant within the congregation's make up
- Identified potential targets of opportunity
- Established priorities
- Set timelines
- Formed teams based on giftedness and relational compatibility

Strategic elements were included at every level of the intervention. The integrative nature of the approach came into play when, through gathered intelligence and correct assessment, the best possible and most promising methods were determined and utilized.

The ability of the USA to wage war has historically developed respect for the ability of American military forces. In modern warfare, battles are fought before the eyes of the world in real time. New expressions associated with war were introduced into the American lexicon. "Shock and Awe," for example, became descriptive of the type of warfare that overwhelms an enemy and is quick, decisive, and effective.

After thirteen years of war in one region of the world or another, civilians have become familiar with some of the terminology used by military forces such as: targets of opportunity, precision bombing, weaponry, weapons of mass destruction, chemical and biological weapons, air support, sorties, engage, and a whole host of others. In our instant, around the clock society, news coverage tends to run twenty-four hours, with networks competing for the best coverage and the most up-to-the-minute breaking news. The terms of war have become part of the cultural dialogue.

Due to military proficiency, USA influence around the globe has been consistent for decades. On numerous occasions, military forces have had the opportunity to see how quickly forces made progress into enemy territory, confront resistance, and defeat the enemy.

The language of warfare is not foreign to the believer. Regardless of theological position on war or political affiliation, we cannot deny the biblical references and uses of war as metaphors. It is not new. It is ancient, but once again relevant. The Church is in a cosmic struggle of good versus evil. Believers have a mission, the outcome of which has greater implications for humankind than any war fought to date. It has greater consequences than any war that will ever be fought. The Church is on a mission to fight for the souls of men, women, and children worldwide.

## The Mission

Adrian Hastings writes:

In truth it is because of the mission that there is a Church; the Church is the servant and expression of this mission. The mission consequently dictates the nature of the Church and as far as the Church fails to live up to the demands of mission, it is effectively failing to be the Church. In this perspective, it is misleading to say that the purpose of the mission is the expansion of the Church; in the fullest sense of mission, the Church cannot possibly be its end. Rather, it is the Church called into being by mission for the sake of salvation.[71]

Scripture is full of the language of war as a metaphor for spiritual realities. Given America's history and the way in which military language has become a normal part of American dialogue, creating an evangelistic focus using the terminology of warfare may communicate effectively to audiences. Scripture provides ample examples of passages in which language of warfare is used as a description of a Christian's response to evil. Such language is not new to the Christian community. A long-standing example is the Salvation "Army," a successful evangelistic and humanitarian organization since 1865.

Ephesians 6:11-18 clearly connects the Christian mission to warfare when it instructs believers to:

*Put on the full armor of God, so that you can take your stand against the devil's schemes. For our struggle is not against flesh and blood, but against the rulers, against the authorities, against the powers of this dark world and against the spiritual forces of evil in the heavenly realms. Therefore, put on the full armor of God, so that when the day of evil comes, you may be able to stand your ground, and after you have done everything, to stand. Stand firm then, with the belt of truth buckled around your waist, with the breastplate of righteousness in place, and with your feet fitted with the readiness that comes from the gospel of peace. In addition to all this, take up the shield of faith, with which you can extinguish all the flaming arrows of the evil one. Take the helmet of salvation and the sword of the Spirit, which is the word of God. And pray in the Spirit on all occasions with all kinds of prayers and requests. With this in mind, be alert and always keep on praying for all the Lord's people.*

The imagery of the text is that of a soldier suited for battle. It is communicated to Christians because they would have understood the context. A military presence was an everyday occurrence to them. They would have been aware of the uniform and armament of soldiers and grasped the metaphor. It is just as valid today as it was then. The weaponry has, of course, changed, but the metaphor is a valid tool for communicating a biblical truth.

War is part of life and will continue to be until the Lord returns. Wars have to be fought. Competent, well-trained, and equipped warriors have the advantage. An organized and skilled army that goes against a less prepared foe should prevail. The Church must prevail over her enemy. The enemy must be properly understood. Believers are not at war with nonbelievers. Instead, people are often in the grip of the enemy and the Church serves to point them to Christ who offers freedom, forgiveness, and restoration.

There are casualties of war even in the spiritual sense. People are hurt, lose their way, become trapped in sin, and become captives. War is dangerous. It seems as if many believers today do not realize the nature and extent of the spiritual conflict. Spiritual warfare is every bit as real as the type seen playing out on the news.

Some Christians would become more engaged in the battle if they had the right tools, a good understanding of how to proceed in an effort, proper preparation, strong support, and a well-defined plan of approach. Others may choose to hunker down or retreat until the Lord comes. They miss the excitement, challenge, and the opportunity to be effective for the Kingdom. We need also to consider the cost of doing nothing or settling for stale ineffective methodologies. There are potential eternal costs in the form of lives not touched by the gospel, and costs among the body as their spiritual muscle atrophies.

What may have been lacking among some churches was a thorough strategy that considered specific conditions. A variety of the standard approaches are occasionally attempted with little or no result. Church budgets should include money for evangelistic services. The attendees tended to be believers who responded out of a sense of duty, but with diminishing returns.

## Integration

The STEP system integrates approaches that, when utilized, provide one more way to look at and frame the evangelistic work that believers are to accomplish. The innovation is not in the methodology or in offering yet one more technique. It is, instead, a system that forces the participants to determine the unique evangelistic opportunities and methodologies that worked best for them with purpose and an honest assessment of giftedness. The approach aided in developing a personal understanding of the natural evangelistic bents among participants and a corporate understanding of how to apply them for maximum impact.

Some of the evangelistic approaches in use today are the equivalent of lances on horseback going against tanks. Without the appropriate weaponry, the effort will be in vain, the casualties high, and the damage to the enemy inconsequential.

Each church can do a better job at discerning the time and using greater wisdom to defeat foes, which consist of any force or idea set against an effective communication of the gospel message. The

Church is fighting an enemy that uses every type of technology to his advantage, while some segments of Western churches limp along with a nostalgic point of view that taints their missional effectiveness in light of existing cultural realities.

Churches have a mission problem and the barrier of a poor image. Each chink in the collective armor of the Church is broadcast in the media to diminish credibility further. However, the image of the Church can be turned around. The best approach is to remain focused on the efforts that hold the most promise and rely on the Lord to build His Church. It may require a shift in how the central message is communicated to the masses. Knowing the audience and what they connect with will go a long way toward greater market penetration. As the metaphor of strategic warfare is embraced and strategy or technology employed, evangelistic efforts will soar to a new level.

## Spiritual Freedom

There is no more noble a cause than a war for the spiritual freedom of the souls of men, women, and children. From a scriptural point of view, there is no option. Believers are called to be witnesses for Christ. In the last century, many within churches across the nation formed their understanding of our role in society through the hymns of the church. One such hymn brilliantly portrays the nature of the mission:

> Onward, Christian soldiers, marching as to war,
> With the cross of Jesus going on before.
> Christ, the royal Master, leads against the foe;
> Forward into battle, see His banners go!

> At the sign of triumph Satan's host doth flee;
> On then, Christian soldiers, on to victory!
> Hell's foundations quiver at the shout of praise;
> Brothers, lift your voices, loud your anthems raise.

> Like a mighty army, moves the church of God;
> Brothers, we are treading, where the saints of trod.
> We are not divided, all one body we,
> One in hope and doctrine, one in charity.[72]

Jesus Christ calls believers to be witnesses in the world. Our identity is connected to the mission. The source of our Power is the greatest ever known. However, many churches try to take on the enemy without the empowerment of the Holy Spirit of God. The best piece of equipment is the work of the Holy Spirit in the lives of the believer. He reserves the greatest show of strength for the soldiers who need it most. They are the soldiers on the frontlines of battle.

The extent of the sacrifices of those on the frontlines should never be underestimated. The slings and arrows are reserved for those who put themselves in harm's way. The frontline forces receive the attention of the enemy who is bent on undermining them in any way possible. He does not follow accepted rules of engagement. The enemy is ruthless, cunning, and cruel. There will, of course, be casualties and collateral damage in the form of tired warriors, soldiers who fall into temptation, and innocents who get hurt in the process. However, those who persevere in the faith become the real heroes.

Some churches may fear engaging the enemy because they feel so powerless and ill-equipped. God asks for faithfulness; and to the degree that is accomplished, the church may march vigorously forward into battle. He will be there with the power, supplying each one with the right weaponry for the right time.

We cannot over emphasize the need to use every possible strategic tool to achieve mission results. The church committed to Kingdom impact through strategic evangelism, will be a congregation ready for the fight, fighting with spiritual tools; and at strategic times, the tools of the world. The Christian leader realizes that while we fight against principalities and powers, the battle is often played out and manifested in society, right before our eyes. At all times, they are committed to alignment with the direction, will and purpose of God. The Holy Spirit is the guide, and programs and agendas yield to His direction. Pray, seeking out the face of God constantly, is the primary means of doing battle, and making certain you are engaged as the Lord wants you to be. Alignment is first in any strategy.

Nothing is accomplished without prayer. The battles are waged against principalities and powers. Our primary weapons of warfare

are spiritual in nature. Prayer is the driving force upon which the hand of God moves. We are in alignment with His purposes when we share our faith. Alignment is where the supernatural power of God manifests. It is here that *"all we ask or imagine"* becomes reality (Ephesians 3:20).

The Church has a biblical mandate to communicate the gospel to humanity. Churches are not being as effective in the cause as they could be. It is time to realize the significance of cultural issues and adopt strategic approaches to evangelism that helps bring people to Jesus Christ. There are multitudes of historical examples illustrating the advantage of a well-thought-out and tremendously executed plan.

The metaphor of warfare is appropriate for believers to embrace. Some people may bristle at the comparisons and the terminology. Others may misunderstand the idea, assuming that pre-Christian people are being viewed as the enemy. However, the enemy is the one holding them captive. Our adversary is Satan and his minions. The church is to be motivated by a love for Jesus Christ and those who need to know Him as Lord and Savior. Taking the mission seriously and committing to a cause greater than ourselves requires a mobilized force.

## Step One Strategy Overview

This process follows a series of pastoral messages calling the Body of Christ to function in their biblical role as a royal priesthood of believers.

A congregation that has not been equipped or challenged to view themselves as part of the priesthood of believers will leave work to the pastor. Already within the household of faith is the notion that the role of the pastor is to feed them, over and above the call upon their lives as servants to Christ, functioning within the context of a mission. At the close of the sermon series related to this issue, adult members of the congregation complete and hand in the questionnaire after the service to minimize incomplete or missing forms.

A small percentage may desire to participate and respond to the call to engage. Accept whom the Lord provides. Keep in mind that the impossible becomes the possible, not because of our limitations, but because of the abundance of blessing and provision of God to open recipients.

The average congregation in the United States is relatively small. Small congregations face some challenges that are multiplied because of the size and the shortage of active participation on missional objectives. The 80/20 rule in the context of a small church is more impactful than in a larger church. The pool of labor is smaller. Furthermore, the church demographics may impact the pool of engaged participants through age distribution. Many smaller congregations have older members. While that in and of itself is not a negative, it may impact the mission objectives. Smaller congregations who have not given attention to the evangelistic call of the church may have suffered over time and lost a cross section of younger members, thus decreasing the number of those who could help the church grow evangelistically.

It is natural to wonder how a mission is to be accomplished when the challenges are great and the numbers are few. The reality is, no mission effort will be successful if there is not enough spiritual support. Spiritual support is born out of prayer. Execution of a plan is highly contingent on the spiritual dynamics, over and above every other consideration and factor. The best plans with the greatest force of labor may enjoy only marginal success if prayer has not been brought to bear upon the challenge.

Plan meeting times when greatest participation can be expected and schedules are best accommodated.

## Checklist: Meeting One

- Invite strong Christians from the church who possess a deep mission mind to participate in the great adventure of Kingdom building.
- Administer a battery of personality inventories designed to give participants and the leadership team a clear understanding of each participant's strengths and weaknesses.
- Identify individuals or people groups that each participant wants to see come to faith in Jesus Christ.

*Step One: Strategic Foundation* 109

- Determine potential points of shared interests. (For example, ask: In what hobbies, interests, organizations, or groups do you have an interest?)
- Determine the level of time invested in potential points of contact.
- If addressing a people group, ask what percentage of non-Christian, unchurched, or de-churched people do they associate with?
- Ask participants how their interests, hobbies, organizations, or groups could serve as evangelistic entry points?
- What potential problems exist?
- How can potential problems be overcome?
- Collect, tabulate, and chart data received.

CHAPTER 5

# Step Two: Targeted Audience

## Intentional Intelligence, Cultural Knowledge

Cultural knowledge and influence are at the epicenter of the process of moving the evangelized church forward. If any criticism can be leveled at some within the church today, it is the absence of knowledge and wisdom relative to the various fragments of culture that exists in our midst, and our apparent unwillingness to influence strategically, with transformational truths. To gain influence and bring transformational truth to our churches, we must reengage humanity at the level that makes us very uncomfortable

Who are we serving and what cultural "language" do they speak? What do we know of our audience, and what relative information do we need to acquire maximum effectiveness in bringing audiences to faith in Jesus Christ?

Step Two includes an emphasis on attitude. Specifically, the apostle Paul's attitude and willingness to do whatever it takes to reach people with the gospel. It speaks to believers and shows us what attitudes should exist and what should willingly be embraced: *"To the weak I became weak, to win the weak. I have become all things to all people so that by all possible means I might save some"* (1 Corinthians 9:22).

This step is an examination of three primary areas of consideration:

1. A review of strategies for gathering information.
2. A determination of best possible options from the cross section of potential audiences.

3. Examples from other sources. The examples serve as primers to lengthier discussions by participants on ideas and concepts unique to the organization. It is not suggesting that the concepts discussed are the best methods. They are examples only to prime the pump and create an environment of exploration. These practices can help break free of tired ideas and fall-back safety positions.

The ability to gather critical information relevant to an evangelistic initiative is part of the process in determining the viability of the initiative. If needed information cannot be obtained through reasonable means, the opportunity may be dismissed.

Step Two offers an introduction to various methodologies for information gathering. The basics are introduced here, with more aggressive strategies developed in coaching steps. Successful operations depend on good information. Understanding the audience is helpful in formulating the appropriate strategy. It may be necessary to acquire more information about some groups over others. The characteristics and traits commonly found among subcultures or interest groups may vary considerably. Some groups may be relatively simple to understand while others have very complex and distinctive layers.

The most obvious means of gathering information is from special interest websites. There are nearly 1 billion websites now, and information about groups, interests, connecting points, and much more, is at your fingertip. Social media has risen to another level in the culture, and offers a multitude of ways in which to connect and find pertinent information. Facebook is the vehicle of the day, but continued development and opportunity for other mechanisms will rise to the forefront of social exchange. Interviewing people associated with a potential evangelistic focal point is also helpful.

However, there must be caution in retrieval of information. While our purposes are redemptive in nature, they could be interpreted as something other than genuine. We must be sensitive to that possible perception. Searches should be generic information gathering, not a means of intrusion into the lives of specific people. Most people volunteer information about areas of interest.

In *Building a Contagious Church,* Mark Mittleberg catalogs the approaches of a number of different churches for each of the evangelistic categories they use. Those materials were used in the process. In the following style sections, Mittleberg's categories have been summarized and presented.

## Confrontational Style

One church offers a "Mugging Ministry" in which visitors receive a coffee mug filled with items that have the church name on them. Another church did a "Direct Touch Ministry" in which the church surveyed area homes to ascertain the level of involvement in a church. Another used "Back to Basics" ministries, where each month people were invited to a meal, hear a gospel presentation, and receive information about the church. Men's Retreats were used by another church to share their faith through high-powered speakers in a retreat setting. A "Thing-a-ma-jig" was held by another church, which is a youth overnight lock-in when the gospel was presented at some point in the evening. Another church is actively involved with Campus Crusade for Christ in which the "Four Spiritual Laws" are shared with college students on campus.

## Intellectual Style

Some churches offer strategic classes and seminars that present answers to questions unchurched people tend to ask. Some churches have also developed a logical presentation based on the responses people give for why they aren't Christians. Steve Brown of Key Life Ministries held "Bring a Pagan" nights during which unchurched people were free to ask hard questions about Christianity, and he would answer them. One church offers a "Discovery 1" course once a month on Friday evenings for newcomers to the church. Participants are invited to "Take their best shot." The team then responds to the questions asked. Another church holds a weekly outreach event in a nightclub where attendees are invited to write down their questions about God on 3x5 cards. The events are appropriately called "3x5 Nights." One church offers a "Hot Topic Zone" within the church's courtyard in which dialogue on hot topic issues routinely occurs. Another church offers a program called "Quest," which is a Socratic, postmodern evangelism course for skeptics.

Other efforts categorized as the Intellectual Style include book clubs, events for skeptics, basic Christianity classes, newsletters to unchurched families, attention-getting book offerings sold in secular bookstores, Internet chat rooms, Internet ministries to those interested in Internet pornography, and Internet resources for people seeking to gain knowledge about apologetics. Two such sites are www.crossrds.org and www.xenos.org.

## Testimonial Style

One church offers a Saturday evening service called "The Seven" in which testimonials are a routine part of the event. Another church uses video to present testimonies during a service. "Straight Talk" is a ministry geared to executives in the community that features a lunch and a talk by a high-profile Christian. "Strategic Saturdays" is a men's breakfast that is widely advertised and features testimonies of faith. One church uses testimonies at every event. Some churches put testimonies into print and circulate them. Another church utilizes their website to post testimonials of overcoming common roadblocks to faith.

## Interpersonal Style

Some churches offer small groups in people's homes so unchurched people are more likely to attend. Others use "Matthew Parties" in the form of formal banquets, block parties, sports-oriented gatherings, private dinners, and the like.

"Fast break" is one church's ministry to executives in the community who gather for lunch, interesting conversation, and drawings for restaurants, theaters, and sporting events. Another church provides videos to its members to pass out to their non-churched friends. College age students are targeted by a "New Home" ministry of a church where students are invited to spend time with a loving family from the church. Other opportunities include fitness classes, a couple's dessert night, "Punch or Tea" events that include Pay-Per-View boxing night for men, and a tea party for women.

## Invitational Style

The Alpha Course is an invitational approach example. A Sunday service at noon to catch the late risers is another. One church holds "summits" where churched friends and relatives invite unchurched men. A discussion of faith is included in the summit. Christmas pageants and "Love Thy Neighborhood" invitational efforts are also done by churches. Another church holds its meeting in a theater. Budgeting seminars, Super Bowl Outreaches are further examples of what some churches are doing to evangelize.[1]

Step Two continues with a review of the previous week's findings. A discussion follows in which the participants draw preliminary conclusions about potential evangelistic opportunities. Ideas included in Step Two help participants consider their own environment, uniqueness, and opportunities available in their context, enhancing the brainstorming step.

## Information Gathering

Step Two then moves to a discussion on strategies for gathering a wide variety of information, or "intelligence," on the proposed audience. It is stressed that successful operations depend on credible information. Gaining an understanding of the audience to be reached will be helpful in formulating the appropriate strategy. It may be necessary to acquire more information about one group than it would another. Obviously, some members will already have specific people with whom they have an existing relationship through a shared point of interest. There may be no need for extensive information regarding some of those specific audience a team member wants to see come to faith in Christ.

Other approaches, may be more tenuous in the strength of relationship, and be predicated on a common connection. The Masons for example, have a superior form of relationship built upon common bonds. A fellow Mason may not need extensive research in order to lead a friend to Christ. He would, however, want to know as much about that individual as possible, which in that context, is not difficult.

Participants are informed that the key to success is having as much information as possible about the challenges they face. Moving into hostile "enemy" territory to gather intelligence about the subculture and establish strategic alliances is helpful.

Witchcraft, for example, is growing and increasingly more open. Some communities have witch covens that are active and practice publicly. Finding locations where supplies are purchased, social gatherings occur, or events are held is not difficult. Befriending people whose belief is not like our own is traditionally a very normal practice for Christians. An audience can be successfully reached by spending time with those who are different from us.

It is optimal and preferable to send someone who has an ability to speak the language of the practitioner. The objective is to gather as much information about the people group or organization as possible from within the group. Motorcycle enthusiasts, for example, have a unique subculture of their own. They speak a type of language unique to them. They often have interests, wants, and desires that are satisfied by their involvement with the motorcycle subculture. They even have a clothing preference.

It is important to the process that participants understand the importance of gaining insight into the potential evangelistic areas. Knowing the likes and dislikes of a potential group improves chances of success and minimizes waste of time and resources.

Let's take an example from one event for motorcyclists. A nationally known hard rock group was giving a concert. The event was a benefit and drew hard-core bikers from the "Pagans" and "Hell's Angels," as well as a group of Christian bikers all mixed together in the crowd. Going into that arena was an education—not one into which the typical pastor would step. That method could yield significant insight into the likes and dislikes of motorcycle enthusiasts. The objective was to find out what drew them together; and when together, how might a gospel message best be communicated? Would it make sense to verbalize it to the group? This is an example of an intelligence-gathering approach that may be needed to impact a specific audience.

Common interests can draw a crowd of the widest variety as long as there is one common thread among them. Another event example is attending a tattoo party. On that fact-finding mission, a good number of unchurched people were directly introduced to the gospel. Some of them could not believe that a minister would be there. But two of the people at the "party" were in church the following Sunday, which reveals the need to break barriers and influence target groups ordinarily left untouched by evangelistic strategies.

Breaking down barriers and stepping outside the box of typical evangelistic targets opens the field of possibilities. The church willing to be bold, along with the people willing to engage at another level, can have significant impact in spreading the gospel through affinity groups and subcultures. The issue is knowing what arena to step into to influence souls and move them toward a relationship with Christ.

I hold to the conviction that Jesus would be in many places the average Christian would not go. Some will not go out of fear. Some will not go out of a particular variety of self-righteousness. Some of it is ignorance, and some is because churches have been preaching a different gospel and lost touch with the heart of the message. Gaining information from firsthand exposure is invaluable. Those assumptions lie at the heart of the strategic and integrative approach.

## Pertinent Demographics

Participants are challenged to think about options in gathering information on potential target groups. One way to understand the subculture is through the merchandising efforts of those marketing goods and services to that unique audience. Magazines are a good source of behavioral information. Anyone wishing to fit in with certain groups must look the part and speak the language.

Martial arts is a growing area of interest in the nation. Participation in martial arts is on the rise. There is an abundance of Eastern influence in that particular subculture. Understanding Eastern thought might help connect people with an interest in that area. All those considerations provide a clear picture of specific target groups and further aid in determining the best or most promising target on which to focus attention.

A wide variety of sporting interests also have unique characteristics, interests, likes, and dislikes. Most general information about any subculture is easily gathered. That goes for areas of interest ranging from basketball to witchcraft. The evangelistic efforts of a church are advanced by understanding the unique attributes of the subculture. Far too often, people try to evangelize without understanding anything about the people they are trying to reach, or the group dynamics that are part of the subculture.

Step Two requires a focus on gathering pertinent information. In subsequent STEPs, a grid is completed that increases in usefulness with a thorough gathering of solid information for target groups.

Information like spending habits, lifestyle preferences, economic status, gathering points, common characteristics and traits of the subgroup should be determined. Certain websites can be helpful as well in the information-gathering phase. The Nazarene Church has done extensive demographic research for their churches around the country. Information is available at map.nazarene.org to anyone free of charge.[2] The demographics will include housing types, income levels, education levels, family units, ethnic considerations, and projected growth patterns. All of that information is free and incredibly useful in determining the immediate area and opportunities within it for ministry. Again, information helps determine feasibility in target group selection. There is no project without good information.

| Potential Audiences | Option 1 | Option 2 | Option 3 | Option 4 | Option 5 | Option 6 |
|---|---|---|---|---|---|---|
| DESCRIPTION | | | | | | |
| POTENTIAL ROAD BLOCKS | | | | | | |
| IMPACT POTENTIAL | | | | | | |
| LABOR INTENSITY | | | | | | |
| AVAILABILITY OF INFORMATION | | | | | | |
| UNIQUE STRENGTHS | | | | | | |
| INHERENT WEAKNESS | | | | | | |
| MISC. | | | | | | |

When the collaborative completion of the Step Two: Potential Outreach Grid is accomplished, participants are asked to consider the evangelistic style, potential roadblocks, potential impact, labor intensity, best intelligence to date, unique strengths, inherent weaknesses, and any additional miscellaneous information that could be helpful.

## Step Two Strategy Overview

This phase of the strategy may meet with philosophical resistance. Some people will not want to view a spiritual issue as something reduced to a humanistic strategy. It is imperative that all understand the importance of hearing from God in the process. It is equally important to grasp the gift that is ours by design, in the form of intelligence, which we are called to use for redemptive purposes.

## Checklist: Meeting Two

- Review the first meeting findings.
- Review the various methods of gathering information, noting specifically what is available in the public domain on the Internet.
- Discuss people's right to privacy.
- Avoiding negative practices.
- Review styles.
- Brainstorm potential strategies for engagement in either personal or people group initiatives.
- Initial completion of the outreach grid.

Chapter 6

# Step Three: Evangelistic Strategies

## Optimizing Best Options

Based on what you have learned so far, what are the best ways to move your church or ministry forward in evangelistic efforts?

The aim of Step Three is to determine the best options for the group of participants to pursue as an evangelistic outreach. We are to be committed to expanding the Kingdom of God by introducing people to Jesus Christ. We are confronted in North America by a culture of a particular stripe and nature. It is problematically complex. Given the challenges, it is necessary for churches to innovate new approaches to communicating the great truth of Christ.

Clayton Christianson and Michael Raynor, in their book *The Innovators Solution*, catalog the multitude of organizations that have gained market position through innovation. The primary means of gaining market share was through some form of innovation that disrupted particular market segments. Disruptive strategies aided organizations in accomplishing the imperative to grow.[1]

As believers who want to reach the most people with the good news, we operate under the same imperative. We too must disrupt ideologies and notions contrary to Christianity. A precursor to that action is changing our own internal challenges that limit our thinking. It cannot be over-emphasized the degree and extent of years of ideological entrenchment in many churches, and the difficulty involved in dislodging them from our collective mind.

It is our responsibility to dislodge ideologies, practices, and beliefs contrary to Scripture. Part of that function occurs through strong apologetics. Beyond that, however, is the reality that if we wish to advance the gospel, we need to disrupt the current cultural strongholds. Part of the disruption has to occur through development of new approaches. To paraphrase Claudio Feser in his book *Serial Innovators,* cultures and support systems to cultures, are made up of rules. Those rules are both written and unwritten. They are the presuppositions by which people and groups behave, interact, and advance. The Church and the church, also have cultures. Prior to breaking down other cultures through disruptive strategies, part of the challenge is to break the internal culture of our own organizations. To be effective in our mission, there is a sense in which internal impediments to growth need eliminated from the body. To create an innovation culture, we need to encourage "mental flexibility, inventiveness and openness." Cultural change begins with the leader.[2]

> Innovations, even eminently sensible ones, don't diffuse simply because they are right and good. James Lancaster, an English sea captain, tried an experiment in 1601 to blunt the plague of scurvy. In those days, scurvy routinely killed as many as half to two-thirds of the sailors on an average long voyage. Lancaster had four ships under his command, all sailing to India. He gave a daily dose of lemon juice to sailors on one ship. He gave no lemon juice to sailors on the other ships. No one died of scurvy on the lemon ship, but so many died on the non-lemon ships that Lancaster had to move sailors from the first ship to staff the others. This seems like powerful proof of the benefits of citrus juice to prevent scurvy, but the Navy did not adopt the innovation. A century and a half later, a British physician repeated a version of Lancaster's experiment, with similarly impressive results. Still, the Navy did not adopt the innovation. It took another 50 years for the British Navy to wipe out scurvy by providing sailors with citrus, and 70 years for the merchant marine to adopt the innovation.

The Church has the answer to the ills of humanity in Jesus Christ. Innovating new ways to get the answers to humanity is paramount. Our stubborn refusal not to aggressively fulfill our responsibility is every bit as absurd as waiting 50 years to take the action that would have saved lives. We have a greater threat looming before us."[3]

Jeff Dyer, Hal Gregersen, and Clayton Christensen identify practices that are the essence of the innovator's DNA:

1: Associating
2: Questioning
3: Observing
4: Networking
5: Experimenting[4]

Associating draws its strength from those who have the vantage point of multiple disciplines. Synthesizing information from a variety of sources, developing from transferable elements, and forming something new can advance an organization.

Questioning the norms, rules, and operational presuppositions can help us break free of restrictive thought patterns that squelch innovation. The leader should be always looking, observing, watching, analyzing, and synthesizing. We gain insights from others. Cross pollination is not only an integral component of nature, it is essential to our development in critical areas.

The desired outcome of the step is a firmly planted understanding of best options for the participants. To arrive at that understanding, the group should utilize the possible evangelistic opportunities from the brainstorming step, and engage in what author Gary Harpst calls the "Hundred Point Exercise."[5] Each participant is given 100 points and then asked to assign a point value to the ideas or opportunities that best represent viable options in their minds. The totals are tabulated and the ideas or opportunities given the greatest number of points are chosen to be the methods through which to evangelize. From there, the field is narrowed down further. The top five choices represent the collective input from the group with the greatest interest and promise for success.

## A Good Fit

The strategies employed for success in the chosen field of opportunity will most likely differ from audience to audience. The assessment of the evangelistic team, their interests, disposition, giftedness and the like, will begin to surface and help define the team nuances needed to help ensure success. A good fit with the right personnel matched to the right target group and tactic will optimize potential. Developing the correct tactics is part of Step Four. The right tactic for the specific group of participants improve the likelihood of success in the evangelistic effort.

There is a reality that just sharing the gospel is no guarantee that it will bear fruit every time. A Christian's role is, however, to be a message bearer. The results are up to God and the individual's response. A church can labor to be as strategic as possible, though, minimizing needless floundering.

Life offers many complications that can make the process very difficult. There is no surefire way of reaching every person. The human will is strong; God does not trample on it, and other variables may come into play:

> *That same day Jesus went out of the house and sat by the lake. Such large crowds gathered around him that he got into a boat and sat in it, while all the people stood on the shore. Then he told them many things in parables, saying: "A farmer went out to sow his seed. As he was scattering the seed, some fell along the path, and the birds came and ate it up. Some fell on rocky places, where it did not have much soil. It sprang up quickly, because the soil was shallow. But when the sun came up, the plants were scorched, and they withered because they had no root. Other seed fell among thorns, which grew up and choked the plants. Still other seed fell on good soil, where it produced a crop—a hundred, sixty or thirty times what was sown (Matthew 13:1-8).*

Being aware of those obstacles, we still must move forward toward making wise and well-thought-out approaches so our evangelism is as effective as possible, determining the best evangelistic approach or tactics to use for each of the target groups chosen. Strategies will most likely differ from target to target. An

## Step Three: Evangelistic Strategies

assessment of the evangelistic team, their interests, disposition, giftedness, and the like further ensure a good fit with the right personnel matched to the right target group and tactic.

George Barna offers an evangelistic effectiveness rating scale with a generational breakdown by age demographics for American believers. He lists the various evangelistic approaches and then rates them on a scale from "major harvesting" being the highest and most effective strategy, to "shame on you" being the lowest and least effective.[6] The following are the twenty-two types studied:

1. Lifestyle or friendship evangelism
2. Family evangelism
3. Confrontational
4. Cell group
5. Power evangelism
6. Mass media
7. Mass crusades
8. Affinity group
9. Social welfare outreach
10. Youth rallies
11. Concerts
12. Drama
13. Sports participation
14. Church planting
15. Traditional church services
16. Contemporary
17. Seeker services
18. Sunday school class
19. Church-sponsored events
20. Socratic evangelism
21. Literature outreach[7]

Barna's is not the only listing of evangelistic strategies. Most other lists are similar and could be connected to one or more of this list. Barna further contends that, "The philosophy behind this approach is there is not just one appropriate way to share the gospel with nonbelievers. However, Christians must be prepared to understand different methods of sharing their faith with non-Christians, based upon an accurate understanding of what approaches would speak most clearly to the needs and perceptual abilities of the non-believer."[8]

Lifestyle evangelism holds the most promise across the board with each age demographic. "Power evangelism," which emphasizes the power of God to work in bold demonstrative ways, is also a good choice across the board. However, as would be expected, other forms work even better when targeted more specifically. The top most effective methods for busters or Gen Xers (people born between 1961 and 1981) are social welfare outreach, Socratic evangelism, lifestyle, cell, power, and concerts. The least effective approach among that demographic tends to be a confrontational approach, the use of mass media, and literature outreach. If the target age group is among baby boomers (people born between 1946 and 1964), lifestyle, power evangelism, affinity group meetings, and contemporary seeker services tend to rank highest.

The builder generation (people born between 1901 and 1925) are reached most effectively through friendships and Sunday school class. They are reached least effectively through youth rallies, cell groups, mass crusades, concerts, drama, sports participation, church planting, and contemporary seeker services. Among seniors, friendship/lifestyle evangelism and literature outreach are the highest. Few other approaches are effective and fall into Barna's "bad" stewardship category. Barna further states:

> Highly effective churches are strategic in their evangelistic efforts in another way too: They devote most of their evangelistic resources to reaching kids. Our research shows that a majority of people who accept Christ as their savior do so before the age of 18-nearly two out of every three believers. In fact, a majority makes that crucial decision between the ages of 8 and 14. Thus, focusing on young people is a wise investment of the church's limited evangelistic resources.[9]

An example of an opportunity discovered through a connecting point is the new pastime: scrapbooking. As stated in Chapter

Two, Brian McLaren identified a need for the church to be more experiential as one of the fifteen keys to maximizing opportunities with the postmodern mind.[10] Each of the best strategies chosen was experiential in nature. There is growing interest in the nation with scrapbooking, and more and more women is particular are taking to the hobby. Several women in our field testfocus groups, wanted to use that interest as a point of contact with other non-churched women. This was a great way to bring together a commonly shared interest and a desire to make connections with people to share the gospel. Because participants would be "in their element" in the context of scrapbooking, more focus could be given to sharing the gospel instead of trying to "fit in" properly in a more unfamiliar environment. They also would be naturally able to communicate well in the "language" of the unchurched who attended the event. Ideally, there would be enough people to form compatible teams.

## "Felt Needs"

Step Three is perhaps one of the most critical. An error here can possibly undermine the evangelistic effort and jeopardize success. Deciding on wrong targets with insufficient resources will compound the errors.

The notion of meeting "felt needs" may serve to influence the outcome of the process. That is not bad. Rick Richardson states in his book *Evangelism Outside the Box*:

> Ministries effectively reaching post-modern people realize that felt needs of pre-Christian people are human needs. They are needs for belonging, relationship, community, identity, spirituality, and the experience of the transcendent. If we meet these needs well, we will be meeting the needs of Christians also. Ministries that have learned well how to meet these profound human needs, using Scripture but speaking the language and mindset of the people today, are growing and seeing people come home to God.[11]

Twelve critical guidelines are essential for effective relational evangelism. Without behavior, conducive to building authentic relationships, opportunity for influence diminishes. If we fail to get past our proclivity to look at others with a sense of judgment, we will not be able to establish meaningful relationships upon which to build mutual respect and care. We must not flinch or rush to judgment when we are establishing friends. Nor should we operate under any false pretense. Carefully consider the following guidelines:

1. Find opportunities with people or groups with whom a disciple has a like interest.
2. Engage with the group or point of interest.
3. Develop a deep understanding of the people involved. Observe without prejudice or pretense.
4. Drop all judgmentalism or preconceived notions about the group or people.
5. Drop spiritual indignity and self-righteous impulses.
6. Love them genuinely, deeply, without the expectation that they love you or will respond to your love.
7. Be real, authentically human, and open about your own flaws.
8. Avoid "churchy" language or phrases.
9. Pray for each person privately, frequently, and while engaged.
10. Establish a long-term relationship.
11. Commit to walking life's journey with them.
12. Only when you have loved them and the Lord prompts, share the gospel with them.

## Step Three Strategy Overview

This phase of the strategy is potentially the most laborious. All expectations about completing it in one setting simply will not work. There will be a temptation at this stage, to decide on strategies with which there is some familiarity. That is to be avoided, unless after significant consideration, the best option is obvious. As with every step in the process, it is important to undergird the step with prayer. It cannot be stressed enough how important it is to sense the lead of the Holy Spirit going forward. That is not to say that no action is taken if some of the participants have not heard. There is a degree of yielding to biblical leadership principles as well. Twenty-one strategies are listed, but the list is by no means exhaustive. It is important to explore a multitude of possibilities with an open mind and an eye for innovative possibilities.

## Checklist: Meeting Three

- Review, rate, and refine potential options.
- Consider disruptive options that break the rules of stereo typical choices and predictability.
- Incorporate the powers of innovative DNA criteria.
- Boil down options through the 100-point exercise.

CHAPTER 7

# Step Four: Planned Strategies

## Resource Review, Proper Tools

Now it is time to answer the question: What methods will we use and what resources do we need?

In Step Four, a discussion of approaches begins to form potential strategic measures. The approach is determined by the best information obtained about the specific audience, and evidence that suggests what would or would not work. This step is the lynch pin of the effort. The strategy matters.

It is also the point where poor decisions may be made. While prayer is important throughout the entire effort, now is when a high sensitivity to the Holy Spirit guides the outcome. We often choose initiatives that may seem simple or easy to implement, but our collective minds must be brought under the tutelage of the Holy Spirit. Going off in the wrong direction will disrupt the effort. Yielding to the Spirit and waiting on His direction, will help clarify the steps moving forward.

As with any initiative, a discussion about potential roadblocks or potential problems should also occur in this phase. There are always challenges. Knowing what could occur, and developing an algorithmic response to possible events, can provide clarity in the midst of crisis.

A checklist of responses to potential events will go a long way toward bringing a high level of professionalism to the initiative. It will also give the team formed for each initiative the sense that there is a significant level of preparation and back-up plans should something go wrong.

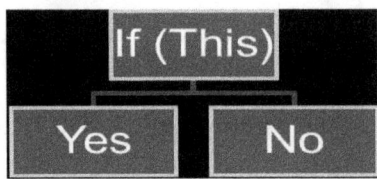

It seems as if there is a common belief that the work of God is simple if done right. That notion may never be spoken, but there seems to be a thread of expectation that rough roads are always made smooth before you cross them. The experience of others does not always affirm that conclusion. The work of God can be difficult to accomplish, full of danger, and destructive of some existing conditions.

For the ultimate example, the passion of Christ was horrific. It was the definitive evangelistic event and included torture, injustice, cruelty, political engagement, and painful death followed by glorious resurrection. Much later in Church life, the Protestant Reformation pitted family against family as bloodshed and violence raged over the issues discussed by Martin Luther. There was nothing easy about changing the course of history and bringing about a redemptive event.

The main question to consider: How will the gospel be shared in the most effective way, given the information available? A study on some existing methods of evangelism and approaches is also covered with the field teams. A group should be prepared to develop timelines for when to share the gospel and in what context for each of the target groups or persons. All possible options must be placed in a matrix with differing plans. A matrix is a listing of options on how different audiences can be effectively reached. Many different approaches can be used to share the gospel. Choosing the right approach for the specific target is important. So many evangelism efforts emphasize the softer approaches, where the church serves others, but does not press the issue of salvation.

Additional key considerations are the theatre of operation, labor, audience, timelines, goals, and objectives for each opportunity. The STEP framework can provide information on obtaining pertinent demographics connected to virtually any subculture targeted for evangelism. Examples from the corporate world on gathering information about present and potential customers are available. Such insights are readily transferable to the local church provided solid leadership and the passion for the lost exists.

The matrix thoroughly lays out possible considerations for implementing a strategy in any given context. The assignment selection, along with the specific team member configuration, is the most difficult. Team selection and assignments of support personnel follow. At this point potential participants submit to a series of evaluative procedures that aid in identifying strengths and weaknesses, which could advance, harm, or limit the mission objective. After the evaluations are completed and reviewed, members are chosen accordingly. Additional guidance is needed in the selection process. Team members should have the following qualities:

1. Spiritual maturity
2. Positive attitude
3. Emotional I.Q.
   - Conscious ability to "choose" emotion
   - Social awareness
   - Self-management
   - Relationnel management
4. Competencies
   - Transparency
   - Adaptability
   - Achievement
   - Initiative
   - Optimism
   - Self-awareness
   - Self-confidence
   - Organizational awareness
   - Commitment to service
5. An understanding of their own values, attitudes, beliefs, expectations, story, decision-making competence.

Jim Collins, in his book *Good to Great,* provides a framework that is also applicable to the process. He includes four stages for development:

- Stage One: find disciplined people. Focus first on who is part of the team, then in what they will be engaged.
- Stage Two: find team members that are disciplined in their thought life.
- Stage Three: find team members with buy in significant enough to commit to difficult, tough, disciplined action.
- Stage Four: find team members with whom the system can continue to build.[1]

Scripture offers insight:

*Be wise in the way you act toward outsiders; make the most of every opportunity. Let your conversation be always full of grace, seasoned with salt, so you may know how to answer everyone (Colossians 4:5-6).*

In the past, one particular method of evangelism would be used in a number of divergent settings. With greater intelligence-gathering capabilities, effective action could take place within any environment—social, political, cultural, etc.

Paul speaks to this issue again in 1 Corinthians 9:19-22:

*Though I am free and belong to no one, I have made myself a slave to everyone, to win as many as possible. To the Jews I became like a Jew, to win the Jews. To those under the law I became like one under the law (though I myself am not under the law), so as to win those under the law. To those not having the law I became like one not having the law (though I am not free from God's law but am under Christ's law), so as to win those not having the law. To the weak I became weak, to win the weak. I have become all things to all people so that by all possible means I might save some.*

Each approach includes a proprietary and detailed strategic matrix of goals, objectives, action steps, and timeline factors for the groups targeted. One group takes longer to reach and develop than another. The matrix helps to keep the team on task with the objectives clearly before them. Once each of the steps has been taken and all personnel are in position, efforts can be launched. Depending on the approach, the evangelistic effort will take place in a matter of days or over a period of years.

The aim of Step Four is to involve the participants in the assignment process of forming the teams. At each step along the way, their interaction and direct input helps to develop "buy-in" to the effort. It is important that participants have ownership over the process. Enthusiasm tends to dry up and commitment levels fade if participants feel they are being forced into a situation rather than determining their own fate to some degree.

Participants have responsibility and a say in bringing about the ultimate goal of the course, which is to achieve an annual 10 percent conversion rate. We must be careful, however, to understand the conversion rate is just a number. Numbers reflect something much deeper and of greater significance. Lives are changed when people come to faith in Jesus Christ. Many of the social ills experienced within a society are diminished when the church keeps a focus the core purpose. When our collective energies are drawn to the severity of the demise that awaits those without faith in Christ, and when we turn that energy toward perpetuating the solution, society as a whole may improve. Of course, we are not so naive as to think that all social ills will go away, but the impact is lessened.

It is all academic if it is not practiced. The STEP system is a tool to help in the process. Establishing reasonable timelines and specific areas of accountability will help in the execution phase.

## Chapter 8

# Step Five: Teamwork

### Tactical Teams, Precision Preparation

How do we best work together?

Formation of the evangelistic teams is completed in Step Five. Given the outreach opportunities chosen and the previous work accomplished to determine evangelistic and team styles, participants now match themselves based on their prior assessment of evangelism style and interpersonal team propensities. Not all participants will necessarily be active in STEP. Some were drafted from outside the group due to their connection to the approach selected.

In the STEP system, there is an inherent applied adaptability. There are often instances where teams will have to act quickly on an issue relative the specific tactics employed. For example, a one time event may require a communication of the gospel before the event expires. That specifically is nothing new to event based evangelism. But it stands in contrast to a longer-term plan of living with a segment of a population over a longer period of time.

Problems and difficulties are to be expected. A certain fluidity in personal resilience is an advantage to the team and the mission as a whole. Adaptability is the key value for each frontline person. Exceptionally rigid personalities will crack under situations that require quick changes in tactics as required by the dynamics inherent in an initiative. Additionally, new ways of accomplishing an objective will manifest. The team must agree to work under the rubric of "Kaizon," which is a commitment to continual improvement.

The leader should strive to develop teams skilled in the following disciplines:

1. Observing mindfully.
2. Considering the opposite of what is "now."
3. Avoiding deadline stress.
4. Calming the mind.
5. Considering the experiences created out of the engagement in the lives of an audience.
6. Stimulating a sense of curiosity.
7. Heightening senses and practicing deductive assessment.
8. Fighting killer words or phrases.
9. Allowing room for fuzziness and getting comfortable with mystery. Not everything has to be spelled out.
10. Looking for unexpected connections.

The desired outcome of Step Five is a force suitable for the unique characteristics of a specific audience. At this point, there may be a need for a fundamental shift in how teams work together and function. In the ordinary course of operations both within the church and outside, the overwhelming governing practices tend to be managed by structured hierarchy. The organization of the local church is a significant issue, and may have to be addressed as the missional objectives become complicated. Congregational structures may tend to prove difficult and actually serve as an obstacle in executing a highly involved and diverse evangelistic approach. Other forms where a clear structure is forced and expected, will have an even greater struggle. So engrained into the minds of many church goers is the structures, traditions, mores and habits of congregations.

Participants complete a review of communicating the gospel by using the bridge illustration. They must each be competent in speaking one on one or in a group if called upon. Since the matrix does not predetermine which evangelistic techniques are used, ongoing strategic evangelistic efforts need a large force of participants while other techniques need only a single individual. The nature of the target group determines these factors.

Part of the process in this phase is to determine the specific evangelistic weaponry needed. For example, an individual attempting to reach a group of motorcycle enthusiasts would probably need to be equipped with a bike. The critical component to the effort is assuring the participants are trained with the chosen delivery vehicle. If the bridge illustration is to be used, all participants need to be trained to use it. If the "Roman Road" or the "Four Spiritual Laws" are used, all parties must be knowledgeable and proficient.

## Step Five: Team Formation

Matthew 4:19 says, *"'Come, follow me,' Jesus said, 'and I will send you out to fish for people.'"* The passage reflects the function of the disciples. Christ makes believers into instruments through which the gospel is communicated. It is interesting to note that an angler often uses a hook and bait. With those instruments, the fisher is able to catch fish. Metaphorically speaking, strategic evangelism consists of using the right hooks and the right bait for the type of fish targeted. There are many different kinds of people. The right hook and the appropriate bait for each particular type of person helps to achieve the desired results.

The following guidelines are helpful to keep in mind:
1. Build and maintain a cohesive leadership team.
2. Create organizational clarity.
3. Over-communicate.
4. Reinforce organizational clarity through the participants.[1]

Teams have life cycles characteristics. The leader and team members are tasked with paying attention to the life cycle of the team. The Forming Phase is where questions of purpose, position, roles, and group dynamics are addressed. The Norming Phase occurs when the team settles into a dynamic that collectively moves a mission forward. Storming is the phase of maximum efficiency. Re-forming in the process of evaluation performances and recommitting to the purpose. Each team member is called to lead at a level beyond the norm. The leader must practice exemplary leadership. They should lead by modeling, leading by inspiring others with the vision of what can be. They should lead by challenging the status quo, lead others to act, and lead by instilling courage.[2]

To be exceptional, there are several qualities and virtues that team members and leaders can cultivate:

- Focus on results
- Promote meaningful change
- Guard your character
- Strengthen interpersonal skills
- Have organizational awareness
- Show respect
- Practice introspection
- Tune in
- Pay close attention to systems[3]

The leader will also avoid the following dysfunctions that can disrupt progress:

1. Absence of trust
2. Fear of conflict
3. Lack of commitment
4. Avoidance of accountability
5. Inattention to results[4]

A team is only as good as its component parts. To have greater potential for team success, it is appropriate that each member of a prospective team be thoroughly analyzed. A combination of resources is available to help determine the strengths and weaknesses of individuals who are part of any given team. For example, it is not unusual to have people take a Myers-Briggs test, a basic and fundamental tool that determines personality preferences. Those personality preferences can further be assessed to determine how they might best fit into a team environment.

For instance, every leader will want to know themselves. Every team will want to know each team member. Through an accurate assessment of test results, the real you will manifest. All of the results can help direct individuals to determine at what point they will reach personal fulfillment. It will also help determine what extent they have matured and have a solid emotional IQ and to what degree they have accepted their limitations, abilities, weaknesses, and strengths. When people are aware of where they best fit in a team given their natural proclivities, a natural energy results. By having closely defined parameters of engagement, people will know what they will be able to say "no" to, establishing a sense of harmony in the working environment—a precursor for success.

It is a foregone conclusion that in virtually every business book dealing with optimal conditions in leading an organization to higher levels of success, matching the right person to the right position is imperative. Having the right person on a team, pushing the right mission in the right way at the right time further enhances the opportunity for success. This scenario can also reduce burnout; one of the best tools for assessing a team is a product of Master Planning Group International. Bobb Biehl did a masterful job at creating a role preference inventory. In addition to that team profile, it is wise to examine of the values and attitudes and insights, confidence and competence of participants and team members. Additionally, knowing the abilities and attitudes toward achievement, along with decision-making insights can better prepare each candidate to understand the critical role in the team environment. Naturally there will be within a team environment people with different communication skills.

It is not uncommon any longer to encounter in American discourse, the propensity to speak rather than listen. A good team member is also going to have good listening skills. Team members will also know their own individual leadership style, their level of trust in others, their level of trust in themselves and how good they are or how lacking they are in building a team. As near as can be determined, ego has to be removed from the team construct.

While we all move in given organizations with a certain degree of ego, there is a sense in which it becomes a negative and dangerous characteristic trait if not harnessed appropriately and the energy related to the manifestation of ego and environment channeled appropriately. We can likewise assess the commitment level of members to not only the team but also to the organization and the mission at hand. How we handle conflict is part of the criteria that can also increase the likelihood of success and decrease failure rate.

More important than any of those, however, is the spiritual condition of the individual team member. The more a person is yielded to the will of God, the more likely success can be achieved in channels for the free flow of the Holy Spirit. Regardless of those human factors and methodologies for analyzing and determining the individual makeup of team members is the presence and the power of the Holy Spirit manifested in each individual and the team as a whole.

There are those in any given organization who are glass-half-empty or glass-half-full people. In times of crisis, the optimist will be of greater benefit to the team. "Darkside" behaviors or works of the flesh brought to bear on a group can significantly decrease the viability and survivability of a group engaged in a mission work. All of these factors can be determined prior to engagement at any level. As much information as possible about individual participants will be helpful in forming teams that can powerfully execute a mission.

CHAPTER 9

# Step Six: Executing Effective Tactics

We have the plan, the people, and the resources, so it's time to start!

## Practical Application

Step Six presents the execution of the evangelistic plans. A further discussion of specific evangelistic assignments along with the projected plan of approach should be held at this point. Each plan includes a detailed, strategic matrix of goals, objectives, action steps, and timeline factors for the groups targeted. One group might take a longer period of time to reach and develop than another. Some of the specific subgroups determined to target will necessitate continued programming for the opportunity to impact and reach its full potential. The process is similar to setting up a business that includes reaching break-even point and profitability as part of the strategy. The matrix helps the participants keep on task with the objectives clearly before them.

## Step Six

Actually getting things done is one of the hardest aspects of any new initiative. It is at the execution point that the best-laid plans tend to lose their effectiveness. Bossidy and Charan write in their book *Execution,* that it is best to identify and correct the things that go wrong at this stage in planning.

The following Scripture—cited previously but important enough to cite and absorb again—for this Step reflects the preparation for battle that Christians must embrace:

*Finally, be strong in the Lord and in his mighty power. Put on the full armor of God, so that you can take your stand against the devil's schemes. For our struggle is not against flesh and blood, but against the rulers, against the authorities, against the powers of this dark world and against the spiritual forces of evil in the heavenly realms.*

*Therefore, put on the full armor of God, so that when the day of evil comes, you may be able to stand your ground, and after you have done everything, to stand. Stand firm then, with the belt of truth buckled around your waist, with the breastplate of righteousness in place, and with your feet fitted with the readiness that comes from the gospel of peace. In addition to all this, take up the shield of faith, with which you can extinguish all the flaming arrows of the evil one. Take the helmet of salvation and the sword of the Spirit, which is the word of God.*

*And pray in the Spirit on all occasions with all kinds of prayers and requests. With this in mind, be alert and always keep on praying for all the Lord's people (Ephesians 6:10-18).*

The aim is to review the execution strategy of the evangelistic efforts chosen and encourage the participants. It serves as the final briefing before any operation begins. As the execution process is underway, there is a need for continued prayer support, adjustments to the strategic plans made based upon the experience and successes or failures, resolution of problems, overcoming roadblocks from external forces or internal issues that any participant may be experiencing, and frequent accountability. Large and complex evangelistic efforts can create more problems that have to be solved.

As needed, there is a realignment of personnel or a shuffling of the team. The execution of the strategies must be prepared for emergencies and committed to being fluid in the process. There are personality types who want everything to move according to plan. Human error is always a factor and can force abrupt changes in the planning.

Based upon the approach, the specific evangelistic strategies can take place over a matter of days, while other strategies may take years before a single conversion is made. Many churches state that they are missional. Far too few cast the net and bring in the catch. It is one thing to learn how to share the gospel, and another thing to do it and execute. Establishing reasonable timelines and specific areas of accountability help in the execution phase. As part of the strategy, the group should determine what expectations are reasonable given the type of evangelistic opportunity employed. Some of the strategies chosen may not be high impact that will immediately lead to a decision for Christ within the target group.

Participants in STEP, and the congregation or ministry as a whole, should be reminded that plans do not always work out. There is a learning curve to the strategic and integrative approach that can provide insight for future efforts. Some information cannot be gathered by any other way but through experience. In the evaluation process, shifts in strategy are developed to improve the outcome in future evangelistic opportunities. If those facts are not understood by people engaged in evangelistic efforts, then unrealistic expectations could form and serve to undermine the entire process.

The evangelistic teams should expect and anticipate resistance. One of the key reasons so many believers are unwilling to share their faith is the fear of rejection. All participants should continually be briefed to understand and accept the fact that rejection is part of the mission. Participants should prepare emotionally and spiritually for resistance. That is easier for some and more difficult for others. A church must understand the enemy will stop at nothing to keep the gospel from having a positive impact in people's lives. In an effort to foster confidence and significant, deep preparation, the Christian Leadership Academy (CLA) offers ongoing courses on apologetics, team building, leadership development, and outdoor experiences designed to test the mental and emotional limits of those desiring even greater spiritual fitness. (See Appendix A for a full description of CLA.)

Those who follow Christ and become bearers of the gospel will most likely collect battle scars. Jesus said, *"Remember what I told you: 'A servant is not greater than his master.' If they persecuted me, they will persecute you also. If they obeyed my teaching, they will obey yours also. They will treat you this way because of my name, for they do not know the one who sent me"* (John 15:20-21).

The arena of missional living is not easy. It is a path of challenges and difficulty. We must surrender ourselves to the proposition that it is better to have served at a high level of personal sacrifice than to have let life slip by with little or no Kingdom impact. Step into the arena.

CHAPTER 10

# Step Seven: Review and Improve

## After-Action Review

Now we answer the questions: What went well? What did not go well? What should we change for next time?

Once an initiative is completed, there are needed times of review. Not everything goes as planned. We often need to encourage the participants to continue the fight and "press on" as Paul told the Philippians:

> Brothers and sisters, I do not consider myself yet to have taken hold of it. But one thing I do: Forgetting what is behind and straining toward what is ahead, I press on toward the goal to win the prize for which God has called me heavenward in Christ Jesus (Philippians 3:13-14).

Step Seven includes an evaluation or debriefing of each of the previous steps, and an overall evaluation of the strategies used and the results obtained. Not every target group can always be evaluated. Some strategies are ongoing. The largest and best-developed effort is such a learning experience that it seems unreasonable for conversions to take place except in subsequent efforts when those strategies are repeated with a better-prepared and experienced team.

Step Seven serves to help guide subsequent evangelistic efforts. It is a critical part of the process. Step Seven is also accomplished through both formal and informal channels, and in groups specific to one type of target group and strategy. If enlisting the services of the Christian Leadership Academy, staff will maintain contact and assistance through a consulting program, which can continue over a longer period of time and adapt with and provide oversight and training for additional strategy implementation.

The framework provides information on obtaining pertinent demographics connected to any subculture targeted for evangelism. The STEP system also uses examples from the corporate world on how to gather information about present and potential customers. The overall process also helps to lay out possible considerations for implementing a strategy in any given context.

The aim of Step Seven is to evaluate and debrief participants on each of the previous steps. It is important to get a sense from participants about their experience, areas of difficulty, successes, and opportunities for future evangelistic efforts. The concern for future efforts and the need for adjustments in the process drive the evaluation. Due to the nature of the strategies chosen, some aspects of the debriefings are accomplished informally and in connection with their event. There may be no shortage of frustration—and excitement as well.

Information gathered in this step and from informal evaluations helps guide subsequent evangelistic efforts by giving valuable insight on operational problems and challenges. One field evaluation in particular pointed to the need for a more effective gospel presentation than the one given. Feedback from parents and the team involved both point to a change that must be made in future efforts. An oversight in the planning phase leads to a situation that weakens the attention of the target group at a critical moment. Steps can be identified to take in future evangelistic efforts that would potentially improve the outcome. The planning, execution, and follow-up to any evangelistic effort provides a great deal of critical information. Each piece of information gathered through evaluation pointed to opportunities that will make a difference the future.

There may be a learning curve in implementing the matrix in a local church. Experience in each evangelistic effort is the best way to gather critical data. Some information cannot be collected in any other way except through experience. It is in the evaluation process that shifts in strategy may be identified and developed. Such is the case in some of evangelistic efforts. Leaders who are placed in decision-making positions have to adapt as they go along. Each person who takes an active role may do so with little previous experience. That means they will make mistakes along the way

An honest appraisal of each effort and the results experienced is helpful. The bottom-line measure of effectiveness is in the number of transformed lives. It may just so happen the strategies chosen tend not to be those that provide dramatic results through one attempt. The programs may have to develop over time and create an environment where those in the target group will readily accept the gospel message.

Other strategies chosen can be one-time events, but perhaps none of those ideas will make it through the previous steps. The strategic and integrative approach utilizing the strategic matrix is a significantly different experience from anything done evangelistically in previous years within many congregations. The evaluation portion serves as a catalyst for developing fine-tuned strategies that may minimize human error and provide a clear opportunity to reach new audiences.

# Conclusion

The Bible clearly conveys the importance of evangelism as a significant function of the Church. There is a connection between the biblical imperative and the stagnant growth or decline in many churches. It appears that the biblical mandate has been largely ignored. Evangelism is not given the focus necessary to achieve the results through effective means in reaching people for Jesus Christ. Competing values, a lack of cultural savvy, and an absence of strategic initiatives designed to target specific segments of the population in a language with methodologies best suited to the target groups, are all factors that contribute to marginal conversion growth rates.

Leadership is critical to evangelism. Significant structural issues within the local church impede the evangelistic effort. The weight of those structural issues hinders the biblical role of the leader within a congregation, which in turn further erodes the use of strategic and integrative opportunities for evangelism. It is common to have some degree of resistance to pastoral leadership authority within the local church. Lost people matter to Christ and must, therefore, matter to the church. Jesus demonstrated an adaptability, cultural shrewdness, and commitment to reaching people to such an extent that the religious establishment acted to counter His influence. The problem has not gone away, but rather intensified over time.

While congregations can make significant impact on evangelistic efforts through critical support roles—such as prayer and financial support—the key factor regardless of the model of contribution is a genuine concern for the lost. Congregations are indeed unique and have a variety of gifts they can bring to bear on a mission.

Without a heart for the lost, they likely will not passionately fulfill their calling.

It was stated at the outset that strategic outreach efforts will result in an increase of people worshiping and living for Christ through the ministry. Success however, is dependent upon the effectiveness of the execution. There are people within the influence of most churches that could be reached by the good news of Jesus Christ, but are not. Why is it not happening? Why are conversion rates low? There are internal, oftentimes strategic failings that contribute to a lack of effectiveness. In order to experience positive conversion growth within churches, the local church must become strategic in its evangelistic efforts, and culturally well informed.

The methodology is based on the assumption that a strategic and integrative approach, determined by accurate research and effective implementation, would most likely increase the quantity of people brought to Jesus Christ through the ministry of the local church or parachurch organization. It was anticipated, and consistent with *Natural Church Development* principles, that participation would be greatest when utilizing what people are already doing by way of hobbies, and interests, with increased evangelistic intentionality. Finding, or developing strategic connecting points, will help determine what type of evangelistic approach is most suitable for the specific operation.

The intervention and the system developed were highly compatible with the traits noted by George Hunter as indicative of effective apostolic congregations. The field group of participants were specific in the target; developed or applied a strategy to meet them, deployed laity to lead in the initiatives, and trained the people.[1] Both strategies employed encouraged active participation with the unchurched, a value Dick Staub identifies as lacking among many Christians today.[2]

Those assumptions are affirmed through the process. It is amazing to see how quickly people volunteer and move when they key into something they are interested in. That alone affirms the validity of the approach.

The strategic and integrative approach to evangelism offers several advantages that did not previously exist. The intervention helps define and focus in areas most that will most likely yield results and develop enthusiasm for evangelism. People are challenged to think a bit more creatively and rise to the challenge as well as find their individual niche in the evangelistic strategies. Participants see a greater connection between their interest and their role as Christians. Less-effective options are eliminated, thus freeing participants to focus in a few areas. Short-term ministry success buys increased credibility. John Kotter notes the importance of short-term wins in creating an acceptable climate for change.[3]

The process is good and the successes offer a glimmer of hope for older congregations. The STEP strategy once successfully deployed, will prove to help in developing effective evangelistic opportunities while at the same time creating a level of enthusiasm among participants. The theological rational for the project was examined and helps communicate God's desire for His people. A study of literature about the church and culture validates the need for the Church to be culturally relevant and connect with the multitude of cultures in their own language.

The intervention positions congregations nicely with a fantastic evangelistic tool that can help them have greater influence in the community for the Kingdom of God. There has been a constant drumbeat down through the years of the necessity for churches to be culturally perceptive and relevant. There is a need for an ongoing sacrifice of time, energies, and even facilities to bring about needed results. The strategic and integrative program offers churches and ministries the opportunity to do just that in a way that assures greater success and stewardship over resources.

Other opportunities for Kingdom impact should follow as long as a vigilant focus is maintained. There is much optimism about the potential of the strategic and integrative approach having impact in a variety of ministry settings.

# Appendix A

# Catalytic Leadership Academy

The Catalytic Leadership Academy is an organization committed to advancing the gospel message through the instrumentality of highly trained, skilled, and competent leaders.

To advance the reassertion of Christian values in a rapidly changing world requires strategic thinking—leading to global action at the epicenters of cultural influence, with excellence in execution within a multitude of disciplines. The Catalytic Leadership Academy is a catalyst toward that end.

## Mission

The mission of the Catalytic Leadership Academy is to advance the knowledge, skills, competencies, and influence of present and potential Christian leaders across a broad spectrum of disciplines with insight and wisdom drawn from key leaders from around the world, to bring strategic advancement of the gospel of Jesus Christ.

## Vision

The Catalytic Leadership Academy is an international force for the effective advancement of Kingdom influence by developing effective, passionate, and catalytic leaders across a cross section of disciplines in strategic locations around the world. It will develop and deploy creative strategies and methodologies across multiple cultural entry points worldwide.

## Core Values

## Christ First

- CLA values alignment with God's purposes above all other considerations.
- CLA values a Christ-centered focus and environment as an organization.
- CLA values an emphasis on grace and faith, over and above practices that tend toward divisive polemics.
- CLA values the unity of believers based not on differing points, but on points held in common.

## Excellence

- CLA values a pursuit of standards of Conduct, Practice, Care, and Quality service that goes beyond excellent.
- CLA values a passionate commitment to expanding the positive influence of Christian values in culture.
- CLA values commitment to the dignity of all people, regardless of race, creed, or national origin, in so far as core biblical beliefs or matters of national security are not compromised.

## Leadership

- CLA values an environment where leaders focus on continuous improvement organizationally and personally.
- CLA values the development of leaders who model and practice positive "can do" attitudes, encourage others to embrace risk, to dream, to believe, to dare and to do!
- CLA values the development of leaders who balance faith and reason with faith as the final factor in the tension between the two.
- CLA values the continuous development of leadership skills and practices that enrich interaction and accomplish the mission with integrity, good judgment, and innovative solutions with calm and clarity.

- CLA values leadership that reflects the character of the person and to those with whom there is direct responsibility.

## Focus

## Build

- To deliver customized education, mentoring, and strategies to reach specifically defined mission objectives.
- To become the preferred organization, recognized for excellence in educating and strategically mobilizing Christian leaders from the full complement of disciplines, with specific initiatives designed to penetrate cultures with the gospel.
- To prepare leaders with the skill sets, confidence, clarity, and resilience to lead themselves, others, staff, strategic functions, and organizations, regardless of pressures, challenges, or impediments.
- To collaborate with other educational institutions.
- To integrate insights from the Academy into courses through published books, articles, newsletters, magazines, and other social media outlets.

## Unite

- To strategically unite Christian leaders toward the end that Christian values, attitudes, beliefs, and expectations gain significant integration into the social fabric and lead to cultural change.
- To bring key Christian leaders from a multitude of disciplines together for lectures, symposiums, workshops, and education related to impactful advancement of Christian influence in all levels of culture.
- To bring catalytic leaders from around the globe to challenge, inform, and inspire other Christian leaders to mission effectiveness.

## Deploy

- To forge alliances with likeminded, kingdom-focused organizations, through which our shared objectives may be achieved.
- To foster the development of enterprise opportunities that can make a strategic impact within specific target areas.
- To prepare leaders to be courageous, bold, ethical, resolute, resourceful, insightful, Christ-like leaders with a fierce passion for the advancement of the gospel through wisdom, love, mercy, and sacrifice.
- To operate in the Americas, Europe, Asia, and the Middle East.

## Statement of Faith

- We believe the Bible to be the inspired, the only infallible, authoritative Word of God.
- We believe there is one God, eternally existent in three persons: Father, Son, and Holy Spirit.
- We believe in the deity of our Lord Jesus Christ, in His virgin birth, in His sinless life, in His miracles, in His vicarious and atoning death through His shed blood, in His bodily resurrection, in His ascension to the right hand of the Father, and in His personal return in power and glory.
- We believe that for the salvation of lost and sinful people, regeneration by the Holy Spirit is essential.
- We believe in the present ministry of the Holy Spirit by whose indwelling the Christian is enabled to live a godly life.
- We believe in the resurrection of both the saved and the lost; they who are saved will be resurrected to life, and those who are lost will face eternity apart from God.
- We believe in the spiritual unity of believers in our Lord Jesus Christ.

# Appendix B

# Scripture Passages Cited

**Introduction**
    Ephesians 6:12

**Chapter 2**
    Matthew 28: 19-20
    1 Kings 18:16-39
    Isaiah 6:5-9
    Acts 1:8
    Acts 2:41
    Acts 8:4
    John 20:21
    Romans 15:18-19
    1 Corinthians 9:22
    2 Timothy 4:5
    Acts 2:47

**Chapter 3**
    Matthew 15:8
    2 Corinthians 5:20
    2 Corinthians 10:3-5

**Chapter 4**
    Ephesians 6:13-15
    John 14:15
    Galatians 2:20

Ephesians 4:11-13
Acts 14:23
Acts 20:28
1 Peter 5:2
1 Thessalonians 5:12
Ephesians 6:11-18
Ephesians 3:20

## Chapter 5
1 Corinthians 9:22

## Chapter 6
Matthew 13:1-8

## Chapter 7
Colossians 4:5-6
1 Corinthians 9:19-22

## Chapter 8
Matthew 4:19

## Chapter 9
Ephesians 6:10-18

## Chapter 10
Philippians 3:13-14

# Endnotes

## Introduction

1. Joshua A. Krisch, "Americans Skeptical of God but Think Heaven Is Real, Somehow," March 21, 2016, Vocativ; http://www.vocativ.com/299168/americans-pray-think-heaven-is-real/; accessed December 15, 2016.
2. SDSU News Team Online Source, "Fewer Americans Now Pray," March 21, 2016; http://newscenter.sdsu.edu/sdsu_newscenter/news_story.aspx?sid=76091; accessed December 15, 2016.

## Chapter 1

1. Wolfgang Simson, The Houses that Change the World (Carlisle, UK: Paternoster, 1999).
2. Adapted from God is Dead: Secularization in the West by Steve Bruce (Hoboken, NJ: Wiley-Blackwell, 2002).
3. Natan Sharansky, The Case for Democracy: The Power of Freedom to Overcome Tyranny & Terror (New York: Public Affairs, 2004).
4. "Online Original Design T-Shirt Sales in the US: Market Research Report"; http://www.ibisworld.com/industry/online-original-design-t-shirt-sales.html;accessed December 15, 2016.
5. Donald N. Thompson, Oracles: How Prediction Markets Turn Employees into Visionaries (Harvard, MA: Harvard Business Review Press, 2012).

## Chapter 2

1. Leslie Newbigin, The Gospel and Pluralistic Society (Grand Rapids, MI: Eerdmans, 1989).
2. John 16:13.
3. Howard Foltz, Healthy Churches in a Sick World (Joplin, MO: Messenger, 1998).
4. Mark Mittelberg, Building A Contagious Church (Grand Rapids, MI: Zondervan, 2000).
5. Aubrey Malphurs, Values-Driven Leadership (Grand Rapids, MI: Baker Books, 1996).
6. Mark Mittelberg, Building A Contagious Church (Grand Rapids, MI: Zondervan, 2000).
7. Gordon Lewis and Bruce Demarest, Integrative Theology, Vol. 3. (Grand Rapids, MI: Zondervan, 1994).
8. Ibid.
9. Ibid
10. F. F. Bruce, The International Bible Commentary (Grand Rapids, MI: Zondervan, 1979).
11. William Barclay, The Acts of the Apostles (Philadelphia: The Westminster Press, 1976),
12. Acts 1:15.
13. Robert E. Logan and Thomas T. Clegg, Releasing Your Church's Potential (Carol Stream, IL: Church Smart Resources, 1998).
14. Millard J. Erickson, Christian Theology (Grand Rapids, MI: Baker, 1983).
15. Ibid.
16. Ibid.
17. Gordon Lewis and Bruce Demarest, Integrative Theology, Vol. 3.
18. Ibid.
19. John Miley, Systematic Theology, Vol. 1 (New York: The Methodist Book Concern, 1892).

20. Ibid.
21. Paul Fetters, ed., Theological Perspectives (Huntington, IN: Church of the United Brethren in Christ, 1992).
22. Ibid.
23. Robert Coleman, The Master Plan of Evangelism (New Jersey: Westminster, 1963).
24. Robert Coleman, Nothing to Do But to Save Souls: John Wesley's Charge to His Preachers (Grand Rapids, MI: Zondervan, 1990).
25. William Barclay, Fishers of Men (Philadelphia, PA: Westminster Press, 1966).
26. Ibid.

## Chapter 3

1. "In Jamaica: Mass Resistance speech at pro-family rally on "gay rights" threat, broadcast live on national radio," December 29, 2013; http://www.massresistance.org/docs/gen2/13d/jamaica-speech-121013/index.html; accessed December 16, 2016.
2. Thomas D. Williams, PhD, "Washpo Attacks Christian Leaders as 'Enemies of Equality'"; http://www.breitbart.com/big-journalism/2016/07/12/washpo-attacks-christian-leaders-enemies-equality/; accessed December 16, 2016.
3. John Clawson, Level Three Leadership: Getting Below the Surface, 5th EditionUniverstiy of Virginia, Darden Graduate School of Business Administration) Pearson, 2011.
4. Ibid.
5. W.Edward Deming, Out of the Crisis (Boston, MA: MIT Press, 1982)

## Chapter 4

1. John P. Kotter, Leading Change (Boston: Harvard Business School Press, 1996).
2. John P. Kotter, The Leadership Factor (New York: Free Press,1988).

3. Larry Bossidy and Ram Charan, *Execution: The Discipline of Getting Things Done* (New York: Crown Business, 2002).
4. Ibid.
5. James C. Collins, *Good to Great: Why Some Companies Make the Leap and Others Don't* (New York: HarperBusiness, 2001).
6. Ibid.
7. Patrick Johnstone and Jason Mandryk, *Operation World* (Waynesboro, GA: Paternoster, 2001).
8. Ibid.
9. Christian A. Schwarz, *Natural Church Development* (Carol Stream, IL: ChurchSmart Resources, 1996).
10. Ibid.
11. Ibid.
12. Christian A. Schwarz and Christoph Schalk, *Natural Church Development Implementation Guide* (Carol Stream, IL: ChurchSmart Resources, 1998).
13. Robert E. Logan and Thomas T. Clegg, *Releasing Your Church's Potential* (Carol Stream, IL: Church Smart Resources, 1998).
14. Ibid.
15. David B. Newell, *Learning to Apply Strategic and Integrative Approaches to Evangelism: A Pilot Project for Crider's United Brethren In Christ Church* (Regent University, Virginia Beach, VA, March 2008)
16. Reggie McNeal, *The Present Future* (San Francisco: Jossey-Bass, 2003).
17. Ibid.
18. Pew Research Center, *America's Changing Religious Landscape* (pewresearch.org, May 12, 2015)
19. Ibid.
20. Reggie McNeal, *The Present Future*.
21. Ibid.
22. Philip Yancey, *What's So Amazing About Grace Study Guide* (Grand Rapids, MI: Zondervan, 1998).

23. Reggie McNeal, *The Present Future*.
24. Ibid.
25. Willow Creek Church, http://www.willowcreek.org/; Willow Creek Association; https://www.willowcreek.com/ProdInfo.asp?invtid=PR20944; accessed December 17, 2016.
26. Bill Hybels, *Becoming a Contagious Christian* (Grand Rapids, MI: Zondervan, 1996).
27. Ibid.
28. Edward Howell
29. Dick Staub, *Too Christian, Too Pagan: How to Love the World Without Falling for It* (Grand Rapids, MI: Zondervan, 2000).
30. Mark Mittelberg, *Building a Contagious Church* (Grand Rapids, MI: Zondervan, 2000).
31. George G. Hunter III, *How to Reach Secular People* (Nashville, TN: Abingdon Press, 1992).
32. C. Peter Wagner. *Freedom from the Religious Spirit* (Ventura, CA: Regal Books, 2005).
33. Ibid.
34. Wolfgang Simson, *The Houses that Change the World* (Carlisle, UK: Paternoster, 1999).
35. David B. Newell, *Learning to Apply Strategic and Integrative Approaches to Evangelism: A Pilot Project for Crider's United Brethren In Christ Church* (Regent University, Virginia Beach, VA, March 2008)
36. Leslie Newbigin, *The Gospel and Pluralistic Society* (Grand Rapids, MI: Eerdmans, 1989).
37. David B. Newell, *Learning to Apply Strategic and Integrative Approaches to Evangelism: A Pilot Project for Crider's United Brethren In Christ Church* (Regent University, Virginia Beach, VA, March 2008)
38. George G. Hunter III, *The Celtic Way of Evangelism* (Nashville, TN: Abingdon Press, 2000).
39. D. James Kennedy, Evangelism Explosion (Wheaton, IL: Tyndale House, 1970).

40. Ibid.
41. Leslie Newbigin, *The Gospel and Pluralistic Society.*
42. Ibid.
43. Leonard Sweet, *Carpe Manana: Is Your Church Ready to Seize Tomorrow* (Grand Rapid, MI: Zondervan, 2001).
44. David B. Newell, *Learning to Apply Strategic and Integrative Approaches to Evangelism: A Pilot Project for Crider's United Brethren In Christ Church* (Regent University, Virginia Beach, VA, March 2008)
45. George Barna, *Evangelism that Works* (Ventura, CA: Regal Books, 1995).
46. Graham Johnston, *Preaching to a Postmodern World* (Grand Rapids, MI: Baker Books, 2001).
47. Ibid.
48. Brian D. McLaren, *The Church on the Other Side* (Grand Rapids, MI: Zondervan, 2000).
49. Ibid.
50. Ibid.
51. George Barna, *Grow Your Church from the Outside* (Ventura, CA: Regal Books, 2002).
52. Ibid.
53. Ibid.
54. Brian D. McLaren, *The Church on the Other Side.*
55. George Barna, *Evangelism That Works* (Ventura, CA: Regal Books, 1995).
56. George G. Hunter III, *The Celtic Way of Evangelism* (Nashville, TN: Abingdon Press, 2000).
57. George G. Hunter III, *How to Reach Secular People* (Nashville, TN: Abingdon Press, 1992).
58. Joseph B. Pine and James H. Gilmore, *The Experience Economy* (Boston: Harvard Business School Press, 1999).
59. "Is Your Company Up to Speed?"; https://www.fastcompany.com/46616/your-company-speed, May 31, 2003; accessed December 18, 2016.

60. https://www.fastcompany.com/; accessed December 18, 2016.
61. John P. Kotter, *Leading Change*.
62. Spencer Johnson, *Who Moved My Cheese?* (New York: G.P. Putnum's Sons, 2002).
63. John P. Kotter, *Leading Change*.
64. Ibid.
65. J. Stewart Black and Hal Gregersen, *Leading Strategic Change* (New York: Prentice Hall, 2003).
66. Clayton M. Christensen, *The Innovators Solution* (Boston: Harvard Business School Press, 2003).
67. John P. Kotter, *Leading Change*.
68. Larry Bossidy and Ram Charan, *Execution: The Discipline of Getting Things Done* (New York: Crown Business, 2002).
69. Michael Slaughter, Unlearning Church: Just When You Thought You had Leadership All Figured Out (Loveland, CO: Group Pub. Inc., 2002).
70. Mark Divine, "What Wolf Are You Feeding?"; Kokoro Camp; SEALFIT, November 2, 2011; http://sealfit.com/what-wolf-are-you-feeding/; accessed December 18, 2016.
71. Adrian Hastings The Construction of Nationhood: Ethnicity, Religion and Nationalism (Cambridge Universtiy Press, 1997)
72. Onward, Christian Soldiers; Text, Sabine Baring-Gould; Music, Author S. Sullivan; 1865.

## Chapter 5

1. Mark Mittelberg, Building A Contagious Church (Grand Rapids, MI: Zondervan, 2000).
2. http://maps.nazarene.org/DemographicsNazarene/; accessed December 18, 2016.

## Chapter 6

1. Clayton M. Christensen and Michael E. Raynor, *The Innovator's Solution: Creating and Sustaining Successful Growth* (Boston: Harvard Business Review Press, 2003).

2. Feser, Claudio, *Serial Innovation: Firms that Change the World* (Hoboken, NJ: Wiley, 2011)
3. Ibid.
4. Jeff Dyer, Hal B. Gregersen, and Clayton M. Christensen, *The Innovator's DNA: Mastering the Five Skills of Disruptive Innovators* (Boston: Harvard Business Press, 2011).
5. Gary Harpst, *Six Disciplines for Excellence* (Findlay, OH: Six Disciplines Leadership Center, 2004).
6. George Barna, *Evangelism that Works* (Ventura, CA: Regal Books, 1995).
7. Ibid.
8. Ibid.
9. Ibid.
10. Brian D. McLaren, *The Church on the Other Side*.
11. Rick Richardson, *Evangelism Outside the Box: New Ways to Help People Experience the Good News* (Downers Grove, IL: InterVarsity Press, 2000).

## Chapter 7

1. James C. Collins, *Good to Great*.

## Chapter 8

1. James C. Collins, *Good to Great: Why Some Companies Make the Leap and Others Don't* (New York, Harper Business, 2001).
2. Ibid.
3. Ibid.
4. Ibid.

## Conclusion

1. George G. Hunter III, *How to Reach Secular People* (Nashville, TN: Abingdon Press, 1992).
2. Dick Staub, *Too Christian, Too Pagan*.
3. John P. Kotter, *Leading Change*.

# Bibliography

Anderson, Howard F. Thesis: *United Brethren Christian Endeavor*. Huntington, IN: Huntington College Theological Seminary, 1962.

Barclay, William. *Fishers of Men*. Philadelphia, PA: Westminster Press, 1966.

Barna, George. *Evangelism that Works*. Ventura, CA: Regal Books, 1995.

Barna, George. *Grow Your Church from the Outside*. Ventura, CA: Regal Books, 2002.

Barna, George. *The Habits of Highly Effective Churches*. Ventura, CA: Regal Books, 1999.

Biehl, Bobb. *The Team Profile*. Masterplanning Group International, 1999.

Black, J. Stewart and Hal Gregersen, *Leading Strategic Change*. New York: Prentice Hall, 2003.

Bossidy, Larry and Ram Charan. *Execution: The Discipline of Getting Things Done*. New York: Crown Business, 2002.

Bruce, F. F. *The International Bible Commentary*. Grand Rapids, MI: Zondervan, 1979.

Christensen, Clayton M. and Michael E. Raynor. *The Innovators Solution*. Boston: Harvard Business School Press, 2003.

Coleman, Robert. *The Master Plan of Evangelism*. New Jersey: Westminster. 1963.

Coleman, Robert. *Nothing to Do but to Save Souls*. Grand Rapids, MI: Zondervan, 1990.

Collins, James C. *Good to Great: Why Some Companies Make the Leap and Others Don't*. New York: HarperBusiness, 2001.

Divine, Mark. "What Wolf Are You Feeding?" SEALFIT, Kokoro Camp, November 2, 2011. http://sealfit.com/what-wolf-are-you-feeding/.

Dyer, Jeff, Hal B. Gregersen and Clayton M. Christensen. *The Innovator's DNA: Mastering the Five Skills of Disruptive Innovators*. Boston: Harvard Business Press, 2011.

Erickson, Millard J. *Christian Theology*. Grand Rapids, MI: Baker, 1983.

Fast Company. "Is Your Company Up to Speed?" *Fast Company*, May 31, 2003. https://www.fastcompany.com/46616/your-company-speed.

Feser, Claudio. *Serial Innovators: Firms that Change the World*. Hoboken, NJ: Wiley, 2011.

Fetters, Paul. ed. *Theological Perspectives*. Huntington, IN: Church of the United Brethren in Christ, 1992.

Fetters, Paul R., ed. *Trials and Triumphs*. Huntington, IN: Church of the United Brethren in Christ, 1984.

Foltz, Howard. *Healthy Churches in a Sick World*. Joplin, MO: Messenger, 1998.

Gaebelein, Frank E., ed. *The Expositor's Bible Commentary*. Grand Rapids, MI: Zondervan, 1984.

Goleman, Daniel, Annie McKee, Richard E. Boyatzis, *Primal Leadership: Realizing the Power of Emotional Intelligence*. Harvard Business Review Press, 2002.

Harpst, Gary. *Six Disciplines for Excellence*. Findlay, Ohio: Six Disciplines Leadership Center, 2004.

Hunter III, George G. *How to Reach Secular People*. Nashville, TN: Abingdon Press, 1992.

Hunter III, George G. *The Celtic Way of Evangelism*. Nashville, TN: Abingdon Press, 2000.

Johnston, Graham. *Preaching to a Postmodern World*. Grand Rapids, MI: Baker Books, 2001.

Johnson, Spencer. *Who Moved My Cheese?* New York: G.P. Putnum's Sons, 2002.

Johnstone, Patrick and Jason Mandryk. *Operation World.* Waynesboro, GA: Paternoster, 2001.

Kennedy, D. James. *Evangelism Explosion.* Wheaton, IL: Tyndale House, 1970.

Kotter, John P. *Leading Change.* Boston: Harvard Business School Press, 1996.

Kotter, John P. *The Leadership Factor.* New York: Free Press, 1988.

Kouzes, James M. *Christian Reflections on the Leadership Challenge.* San Francisco: Jossey-Bass, 2006.

Lencioni, Patrick. *The Advantage: Why Organizational Health Trumps Everything Else in Business.* San Francisco: Jossey-Bass, 2012.

Lencioni, Patrick. *The Five Dysfunctions of a Team: A Leadership Fable.* San Francisco: Jossey-Bass, 2002.

Lewis, Gordon and Bruce Demarest. *Integrative Theology. Vol. 3.* Grand Rapids, MI: Zondervan, 1994.

Logan, Robert E. and Thomas T. Clegg. *Releasing Your Church's Potential.* Carol Stream, IL: Church Smart Resources, 1998.

Laubach, Frank. *Prayer: The Mightiest Force in the World.* Westwood, NJ: Revel, 1959.

Malphurs, Aubrey. *Values Driven Leadership.* Grand Rapids, MI: Baker Books, 1996.

McIntosh, Gary L. *Make Room for the Boom or Bust.* Grand Rapids, MI: Fleming H. Revell, 1997.

McLaren, Brian D. *The Church on the Other Side.* Grand Rapids, MI: Zondervan, 2000.

McNeal, Reggie. *The Present Future.* San Francisco: Jossey-Bass, 2003.

Metzger, Bruce M. and Michael D. Coogan. *The Oxford Companion to the Bible.* New York: Oxford University Press, 1993.

Miley, John. *Systematic Theology, Vol. 1*. New York: The Methodist Book Concern, 1892.

Miller, Ray C. *Into the Fields*. Huntington, IN: Church of the United Brethren in Christ, 1982.

Mittelberg, Mark. *Building A Contagious Church*, Grand Rapids, MI: Zondervan, 2000.

Mittleberg, Mark, Lee Strobel, and Bill Hybels. *Becoming a Contagious Christian*. Grand Rapids, MI: Zondervan, 1995.

Newbigin, Leslie. *The Gospel and Pluralistic Society*. Grand Rapids, MI: Eerdmans, 1989.

Pine, Joseph B., and James H. Gilmore. *The Experience Economy*. Boston: Harvard Business School Press, 1999.

Richardson, Rick. *Evangelism Outside the Box: New Ways to Help People Experience the Good News*. Downers Grove, IL: InterVarsity Press, 2000.

Rogers, Everett M. *Diffusion of Innovations*. 5th ed. New York: Free Press, 2003.

Sullivan, Arthur S., and Sabine Baring Gould. *Onward Christian Soldiers,* Published Musical Score.

Schwarz, Christian A. *Natural Church Development*. Carol Stream, IL: ChurchSmart Resources, 1996.

Schwarz, Christian A. and Christoph Schalk. *Natural Church Development Implementation Guide*. Carol Stream, IL: ChurchSmart Resources, 1998.

Sharansky, Natan. *The Case for Democracy*. New York: Public Affairs, 2004.

Simson, Wolfgang. *The Houses That Change the World*. Carlisle, UK: Paternoster, 1999.

Slaughter, Michael. *Unlearning Church*. Loveland, CO: Group, 2002.

Slaughter, Michael. *Real Followers: Beyond Virtual Christianity*. Nashville, TN: Abingdon Press, 1999.

Staub, Dick. *Too Christian Too Pagan*. Grand Rapids, MI: Zondervan, 2000.

Sweet, Leonard. *Carpe Manana: Is Your Church Ready to Seize Tomorrow*. Grand Rapid, MI: Zondervan, 2001.

Wagner, C. Peter. *Freedom from the Religious Spirit*. Ventura, CA: Regal Books, 2005.

Yancey, Philip. *What's So Amazing About Grace Study Guide*. Grand Rapids, MI: Zondervan, 1998.

# About the Author

Dr David B. Newell serves as the President and CEO of Scotland Campus in Scotland, PA. He was motivated to write the book after significant research in current conditions whithin the average church. David has enjoyed a varied career in the military, ministry, higher education, finance and manufacturing. The combination of experience has culminated in leading a unique international educational organization. He founded the Catalytic Leadership Academy to further study those unique and qualities which show promise in advancing organizations and missions. David and his wife, Linda have three children and six grandchildren.

www.ingramcontent.com/pod-product-compliance
Lightning Source LLC
Chambersburg PA
CBHW071618080526
44588CB00010B/1178